More than Real
Art in the Digital Age

2018 Verbier
Art Summit

Edited by
Daniel Birnbaum
Michelle Kuo

"Thinking
alone
is
criminal"

Karen Archey
Ed Atkins
Lars Bang Larsen
Douglas Coupland
Olafur Eliasson
Pamela Rosenkranz
John Slyce
Dado Valentic
Paul F.M.J. Verschure
Jochen Volz
Anicka Yi

Edited by
Daniel Birnbaum
Michelle Kuo

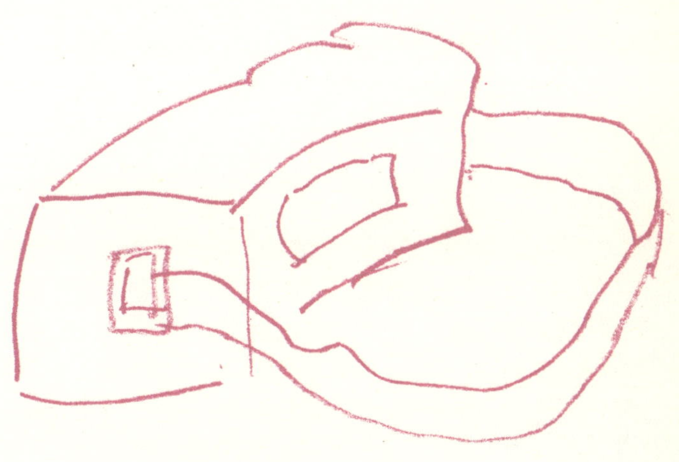

Introduction
Anneliek Sijbrandij

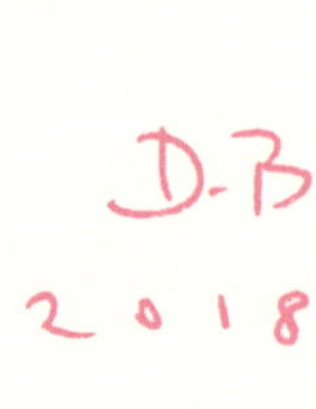

MORE THAN REAL

When you arrive at the Verbier Art Summit, you will have just climbed 1500 metres in altitude, and with each turn winding higher up the snowy mountain, you gain kilometres in visibility, and the distance between you and your everyday life becomes greater and greater.

When the artist Olafur Eliasson arrived at the 2018 Summit, he was greeted by museum director Daniel Birnbaum on a snowy balcony. Daniel's first question to Olafur was, "What are your expectations of the Summit?" Olafur replied that he expected the Summit to be a place for cross-referencing in the cultural sector, immediately adding, "But for me, it's more about coming together, realising that a) you're not alone; but b) we're actually very strong when we are together and when we focus a little bit."

This value is essential to the purpose of the Verbier Art Summit as an interdisciplinary platform for innovation in the art world. The Summit brings together international, innovative thinkers to a beautiful, intimate—almost hidden—site where meaningful dialogue can take shape.

Participants find themselves far away from their typically tight schedules and daily routines, suddenly placed together with like-minded people in a place where they can "focus a little bit." What, then, does it mean to actually *come together* in the digital age, when we increasingly engage only in virtual worlds?

The theme of the 2018 Verbier Art Summit, curated by Daniel Birnbaum, probes the future of the art world (and beyond): **More than Real.** ***Art in the Digital Age.*** Virtual reality, a focal point of the Summit, is a medium that manipulates the very meaning of *coming together*. Olafur is a leading artist who recently worked with this new medium, creating *Rainbow* in which people also participate together, and so Daniel probed on, asking, "What is that strength that we can somehow gain by actually being together?"

Olafur offered in reply, "In general, art has proven again and again that we should not underestimate the boundaries of what is a space and what defines a space—especially when it comes to collectivity and shared experiences." We increasingly participate in virtual worlds, and while these add to our own experiences, we remain first of all embedded in the physical world. So it is meaningful to come together for a three-day event in a small alpine village, surrounded by striking peaks, and feel the snow falling down on us. This is one of our shared experiences, but indeed, we should not underestimate the limits of this experience.

And we certainly don't. The Verbier Art Summit connects thought leaders to key figures in the art world in an inspiring, non-transactional setting, where there is time to stop and reflect, to have deep conversations that may lead to cultural change and innovation. At the same time, we share this experience beyond the boundaries of Verbier with a wider audience, providing free access to the talks by our speakers and live-streaming them on YouTube. This book adds another layer to the Summit's role as a shared experience within the global arts community. By bringing the ideas beyond the Alps and into the homes of anyone with a love for art and innovation, the conversation of the 2018 Verbier Art Summit can be continued beyond its initial three days in the mountains.

A member of our Board of Advisors, the writer and critic John Slyce, thoughtfully concluded, "As art, VR challenges artists to inject human content and concerns into the technology, so that it might not simply take us elsewhere but return us to the lifeworld in order to enhance our lives and transform our relation with an analogue bio-sphere, for which we need to care better."

To move in an increasingly digital world does not make us more robotic, but instead calls for us to become more human, more caring, and more passionate. To me, it is the role of art to explore how to navigate this challenge in the digital age. As you read this collection of essays by artists, curators, academics, and other influential thinkers, I ask you to consider how technology returns us to ask how to care better for our world.

In 2019, the Verbier Art Summit will continue this dialogue under a new theme. By working together with museum director Jochen Volz of Pinacoteca, São Paulo, Brazil, we will explore the theme **We are Many: Art, the Political and Multiple Truths**. We'd like to invite all readers to share this experience with us in

2019, either in person or online (verbierartsummit.org).

It was a true pleasure to work on the 2018 Summit with Daniel Birnbaum of Moderna Museet, Stockholm, Sweden. We wholeheartedly thank Daniel for his innovative curating, for generously lending us his ideas and charm to make an event as creative and thoughtful as he is. We are also very grateful to our Board of Advisors and our Founding Members, who kindly hosted both the speakers and our 2018 Summit Members in their Verbier chalets. We thank all of our other Members, who contributed their time and knowledge to make the 2018 Summit a reality. We also thank our sponsors, the Commune de Bagnes, the Loterie Romande, the Canton du Valais and our new sponsor La Prairie, that hosted an amazing Surrealist dinner together with Charlotte Birnbaum. An enormous thanks to our inspiring 2018 speakers, the artists Ed Atkins, Douglas Coupland, Olafur Eliasson, Pamela Rosenkranz and Anicka Yi, curators Karen Archey and Lars Bang Larsen, virtual reality specialist Dado Valentic, curator and writer Michelle Kuo, neuro-scientist professor Paul Verschure and museum director

Susanne Pfeffer, who contributed so generously to the Summit and this publication. And on behalf of the entire (wonderful!) 2018 Summit team, Sara Alessandrini, Nicolas Bernheim, Fleur Greebe, Alison Pasquariello and Noepy Testa, I thank you for reading this book and for continuing the conversation on Art in the Digital Age.

Anneliek Sijbrandij
Founder, Verbier Art Summit

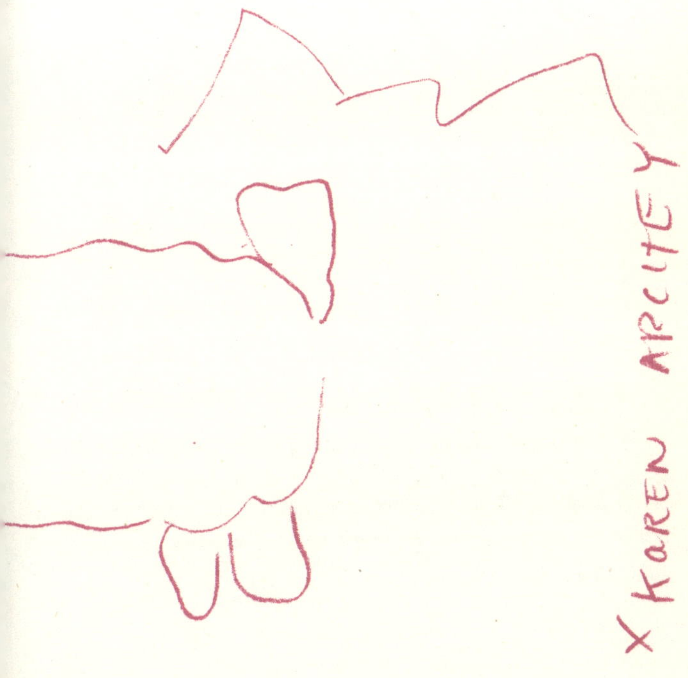

X KAREN ARCITE Y

Premonitions
Daniel Birnbaum

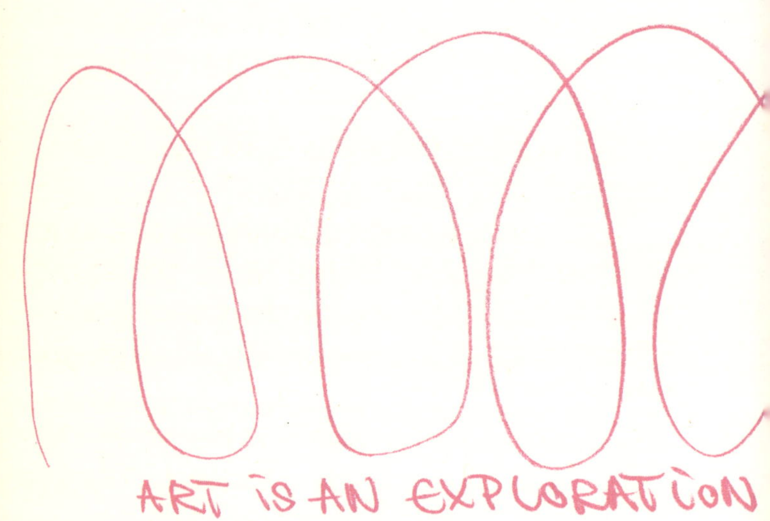

Jaron Lanier, who coined the concept of virtual reality (VR) many decades ago, is still convinced of the medium's importance. In his 2017 *Dawn of the New Everything*, he states what is at stake: "VR is one of the scientific, philosophical, and technological frontiers of our era. It is a means for creating comprehensive illusions that you're in a different place, perhaps a fantastical, alien environment, perhaps with a body that is far from human. And yet it's also the farthest-reaching apparatus for researching what a human being is in terms of cognition and perception."[1]

Lanier has been convinced of this for a long time. And today he is not alone. It seems that once or maybe twice every century, a technological breakthrough occurs that changes fundamental conditions of our being-in-the-world. Quite recently, I asked Douglas Coupland, who has prognosticated some of the most critical generational shifts of our time, to spell out some of the implications of the virtual reality revolution that no doubt will become evident to all of us in a very near future:

DB Some people seem to think that VR, when fully established, will change the way we inhabit this planet—the way we live, work, and communicate with one another.

DC Utterly.

DB Do you think it is a bit like the introduction of TV? Or more like the invention of electricity?

DC Electricity. Life without VR will be intolerable.[2]

Since our conversation was published in an art magazine, Artforum, it naturally focused on the medium's possible impact on the future of art production:

DB Do you think the medium will give rise to a new kind of art?

DC I hope so. Also, remember that when a new technology triumphs, it allows the technology it's rendered obsolete to become an art form. That's what happened with the Internet. It allowed TV to finally make art. Therefore, the next step is for the rise of VR to allow a golden age of internet art, like the golden age of television that started in the early

2000s. When TV first came out, everyone's first idea was to use it for puppet shows. So, I think at first there'll be a lot of echoing of other art forms until the medium finds it legs.

DB Will all disciplines reappear as simulations in virtual space and double everything we have ever considered art, regardless of genre?

DC That would be exciting, and I think it's a large part of what will evolve.

This exchange represented an important starting point for **More than Real. *Art in the Digital Age.*** During the year that has passed since the conversation with Coupland took place, some of the world's most prominent artists have started to explore the medium. Among them is Anish Kapoor, whose VR work *Into Yourself, Fall*, 2018, is a disorienting journey through the human body. In an interview for *Financial Times*, he spells out the possibilities and the risks of the new medium. "At the high end of the scale, the extraordinary effects of sensation can achieve something poetic," he says. "But on the other side, there is the possibility of making something ridiculous, that is not so different from a theme park or a fun ride. The kitsch and the sublime are very close to each other."[3]

This mingling of high and low, the sensational and the ridiculous, beauty and tackiness, seems to be what makes many virtual reality endeavors reminiscent of Surrealism. In his *Surrealist Manifesto*, André Breton named historical figures such as Gustave Moreau, who in his view were Surrealists *avant la lettre.* Other members of the Surrealist group soon added names to the list of visionary precursors, and unsurprisingly Hieronymus Bosch's *The Garden of Earthly Delights* emerged as a key source of inspiration.

The 2018 Verbier Art Summit started with a Surrealist dinner. All the participants were invited to dine at tables decorated with oversized seashells, swords, flower arrangements, giraffes, and artificial pearls. Salvador Dalí emerged with friends on a large projection. This set the tone for the following days of conversations around the possibilities and dangers of new media in the arts. "Never has a medium been so potent for beauty and so vulnerable to creepiness," says Lanier about VR. "Virtual reality will test us. It will amplify our character more than other media ever have."

It was Walter Benjamin who observed a prophetic capacity in certain works of art that allude to technologies that have not yet been developed: "The history of every art form shows critical epochs in which a certain art form aspires to effects which could be fully obtained only with a changed technical standard, that is to say, in a new art form."[4] What could be examples of such prophetic power? It has been claimed, for instance, that certain nineteenth-century novels anticipate cinema, that they are written for a medium that did not yet exist. Emily Brontë's *Wuthering Heights*, one could claim, is written like a film script. Similarly, the branching narratives of Jorge Luis Borges could seem to anticipate hypertext fiction.

Benjamin's essay on mechanical reproduction opens with a quote from Paul Valéry: "We must expect great innovations to transform entire techniques of the arts, thereby affecting artistic innovation itself and perhaps even bringing about amazing change in our very notion of art."[5] Sometimes artists offer a kind of prevision, and when it comes to digital possibilities and the spaces opened up by VR, one can detect premonitions in many places.

German tech-pioneer Thomas Bayrle's early work, I would claim, represents a case in point. Given that some of his best-known pieces were created at a time when no regular person had a computer at home, the anticipatory power of his creations become apparent. Already in the 1960s, Bayrle saw the revolutionary development of technology coming: "Actually I anticipated that something like this would come even in the analogue age, and that someday there would be machines that would do things that at the time I wanted to do, and had to do with the hand."[6] But there are many other examples of art's anticipatory capacities. In some of Philippe Parreno's works, one can detect premonitions of virtual possibilities. In fact, he seems to have created VR works before he had access to the technology. Recently, the artist turned Tate Modern's Turbine Hall into a mesmerizing machine producing light, sound, cinematic effects, and choreography: Inflated fish floated in the air, huge planes reminiscent of Russian Constructivism ascended and descended inscrutably in the semidarkness, and a flickering apparatus seemed to send out signals that triggered reactions throughout the entire museum. There were echoes of Duchamp and Cage. But this expansive machinery went beyond such precursors in scale, as well as in speculative ambition, hinting (as we've seen before in Parreno's works) at a grand synthesis—even symbiosis—of the organic and artificial realms. His vision of futuristic biocomputing materialised as a flagon of yeast whose fluctuations allegedly controlled the colossal orchestration of the building. It's the kind of idea that endows Parreno's most ambitious works with a metaphysical dimension. Parreno's works in many ways liberate the viewer from the common belief that the world is neatly divided in two spheres: us humans and things out there. Time to rethink.

Another artist in Parreno's generation who also creates complex arrangements that seem to anticipate virtual space is Dominique-Gonzales

Foerster. Asked to describe her open-air project at Documenta 11, she lists some of the heterogeneous elements that were displayed amid the shadows cast by the large trees south of Kassel's orangery and where, on hot days, one could see exhausted viewers dozing away on the lawn: "It's a park; it's a plan for escape; it's an extra-large piece of lava rock that's come from Mexico and landed on the green grass; it's a blue phone booth from Rio de Janeiro; it's a butterfly pavilion screening a film inspired by *The Invention of Morel*, the fantastic novel by Adolfo Bioy Casares; it's a rose tree from Chandigarh." On hearing this catalogue of seemingly unrelated parts—removed from their original contexts but arrayed together in subtle tension—one senses that the work is less a particular, circumscribed space or medium than an atmosphere that draws out the melancholy inherent in objects in the world.

Still, one may ask: What exactly is *Park—A Plan for Escape*? A curious sculpture garden, an installation, or an outdoor cinema equipped with exotic props? Probably all of the above, but the project is also a premonition of things to come. In a way,

Gonzalez-Foerster creates assemblages that involve gardens, flower arrangements, and entire cities, often using cinema to alter an urban landscape, whether it is a lush German park or the subterranean maze of a Parisian subway station. In *Park—A Plan for Escape*, a butterfly-shaped pavilion is a kind of cinematic machine, a freestanding projection booth presenting imagery of parks in turn, from films like Antonioni's *La Notte*, Tsai Ming-Liang's *Vive l'amour*, and Resnais's *Last Year at Marienbad*. One gets a glimpse of bodies and faces behind the pavilion's glass, hardly visible during daytime but suddenly entirely visible when night falls. All of this makes no sense in Euclidean space. In many of the artist's installations, this blankness is expressed quite physically, as she leaves large spaces empty. She has captured these dislocations and incoherences with great precision, and in work after work she has recorded lacunae of meaning in places as distant as Brazil, China, and Japan. But ultimately they point at other dimensions, impossible to render visible without technologies to which the artist did not yet have access. Like Parreno's installations, her works are visionary precursors to virtual realms.

Even in the most traditional of artistic mediums, one can find examples of the premonition of virtual realities. The late Michel Majerus never mourned the death of painting or authenticity, and yet his work concerns the very limits of painting's possibility and the kinds of representation associated with the medium. Perhaps more interesting than the introduction of various popular vocabularies into his art—a standard operation in much work today—is the way in which the digital methods of picture production seem to alter the very space of representation itself, producing a strange sense of emptiness and visual dissonance.

This radical discontinuity is the most important feature of Majerus's art. It is difficult to navigate the spaces offered in his works. To an eye not trained in the visual logic of computer games, the space can make little sense. Here, the brain, as Gilles Deleuze put it in a different context, "has lost its Euclidean coordinates and now emits other signs"[7]—signs that are hardly compatible with the traditional conditions of what we call painting, the medium of a certain flatness. With the proliferation of digital technologies, we have become more accustomed to layouts that embrace this heterogeneity, and Majerus is an artist who, perhaps more effectively than any other, has chosen to display and even exacerbate this visual logic. One of his means is the disconcertingly empty ground in which the recognizable elements tend to float. These areas, usually white, seem to distance the components from one another rather than producing a sense of unity. He never used his medium as a field of resolution. Instead, he treated painting as a zone where pictorial elements seemed to create assemblies on the verge of collapse. Painting is an unsatisfactory armature for containing and supporting all the disparate systems he brought to it. Ultimately, it seems clear to me that he was anticipating virtual technologies not yet at hand.

Can art be prophetic in the sense that it predicts scientific and technological revolutions that have not yet taken place? One last case in point: Marcel Duchamp's *The Large Glass*, with its complex geometries that crystallised in a work of art we are still struggling to fully grasp. It is not a painting in the traditional sense but an entirely new kind of artwork characterised by the artist as a "delay in glass". The original version of the work is permanently installed at the Philadelphia Museum of Art. However, the second version–produced by Swedish art critic Ulf Linde in dialogue with Duchamp (and signed by the artist in 1961)–has been at the center of all major Duchamp exhibitions after World War II, from his 1963 retrospective in Pasadena to the major surveys in London, Stockholm, and the Centre Pompidou in Paris. Linde, like many other critics trapped in Duchamp's cosmos, became obsessed with figuring out the secret geometries that he believed to be an important aspect of the work. He found fragments and hints in Duchamp's writings and conversations: "Most people who know anything at all about Marcel Duchamp, know that he was interested in geometry and mathematics. It is therefore puzzling that so little has been written about how this can be traced in his art, even though he himself has clearly pointed out where the first traces are to be found."[8] In one interview, Pierre Cabanne asked Duchamp to explain how he developed the complicated system of measurements in *The Large Glass*, and the artist replied: "The explanation is in Moulin à café."[9]

Linde was convinced that mathematical speculations about a fourth dimension developed by the Cubist group Section d'Ore around 1912 remained a significant key to all of Duchamp's most ambitious works. Linde believed they were secretly linked by geometrical patterns. Philosophical issues, concerning Einstein's theory of relativity and the philosophical speculation of Henri Bergson, were at the center of the *Section d'Ore* group's interests. They were developed in intense dialogue with the mathematician Maurice Princet. Using virtual reality and augmented reality, Damjan Jovanovic and a group of artists and architects in Frankfurt recently created *The Third Glass*—a speculative, spatial-digital object based on Marcel Duchamp's legendary work. I would have loved to hear what Ulf Linde would have thought of this *Third Glass*, a work that takes place in dimensions that Duchamp clearly anticipated but to which he had no perceptual access.

These and other premonitions are what the 2018 Verbier Art Summit explored. For participants such as neuroscientist Paul Verschure and artist/writer Coupland, the new digital technologies are well known territory. For some of the artists—Ed Atkins, Pamela Rosenkranz, and Anicka Yi, say—I think it is only a question of time until the perceptual opportunities provided by VR will be exploited; there are so many aspects of their work that appear to anticipate these possibilities. Olafur Eliasson's art likewise regularly reminds us that we are embodied subjects located in physical space who encounter other bodies. It may thus seem surprising that he already explores techniques that seem to dematerialize not only what is physically given but the viewer's bodily presence as well. *Beauty* (1993), an early work that Eliasson has recreated in several versions, defines the basic parameters that recur in his practice from installation to installation: an emphasis on perception and the viewer's active involvement in the process. Tiny drops of water sprinkle down from a perforated hose, creating a liquid curtain; a lamp sends rays of light through the water to produce a rainbow in the room. The overtness of the technical setup is typical of Eliasson's art: nothing is hidden. When this simple rainbow is recreated in virtual reality–as is achieved in his 2017 *Rainbow*–everything that we thought we knew about ourselves and our perceptual possibilities needs to be interrogated. Are we now more than real?

1   Jaron Lanier, *Dawn of the New Everything.
    A Journey Through Virtual Reality*
    (London: The Bodley Head, 2017), 1.
2   'Wildest Dreams: Douglas Coupland talks with
    Daniel Birnbaum, *Artforum*, November 2017, 195.
3   *Financial Times*, 23 March 2018.
4   Walter Benjamin, "The Work of Art in the Age of
    Mechanical Reproduction" in *Illuminations*, trans.
    H. Zohn (New York: Schocken Books, 1969), 237.
5   Ibid.
6   Thomas Bayrle, *Artnet*, November 30, 2016.
7   Gilles Deleuze, *Cinema 2: The Time-Image*,
    trans. Hugh Tomlinson and Robert Galeta
    (London: The Athlone Press, 1989), 278.
8   Ulf Linde, unpublished manuscript,
    Ulf Linde Archive, Moderna Museet, Stockholm.
9   Ibid.

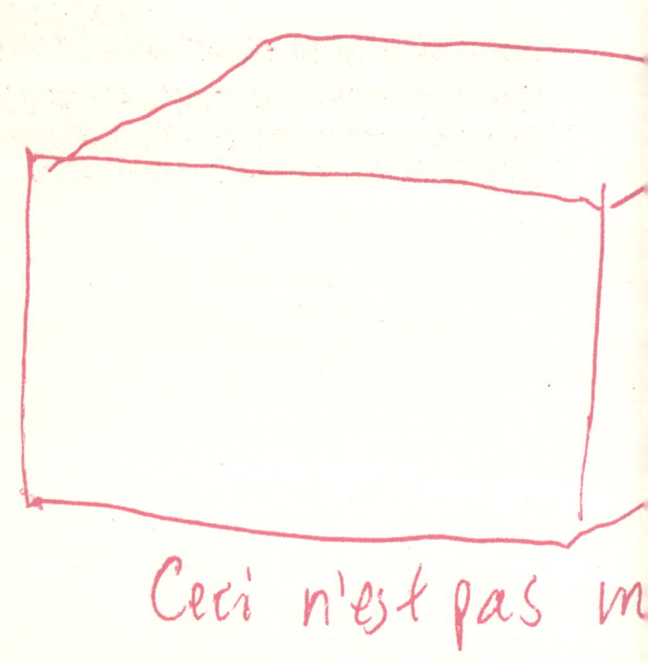

MORE THAN REAL

oite .

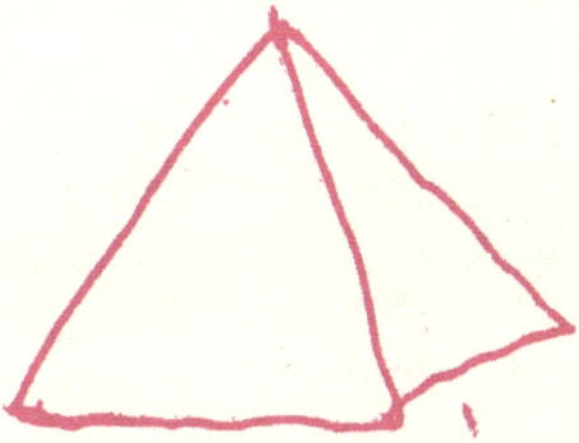

Pas de
pyramide
ici

Mirage
Michelle Kuo

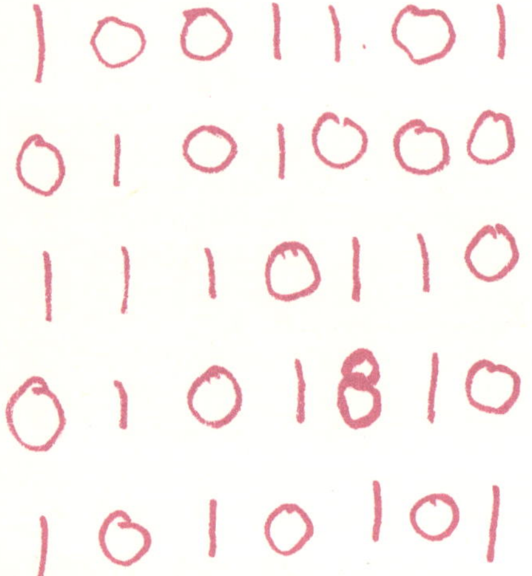

We have long held the fantasy of living in total illusion. Artists have conjured immersive and virtual environments for centuries, in a history that ranges from the eighteenth-century mechanical theater of Philippe-Jacques de Loutherbourg to nineteenth-century phantasmagoria, from Disney's Circarama to holographic video, from surround sound to experience machines. And these chimerical endeavors have often entailed finding new technologies for shaping image, sound, and space. In 1970, for example, the group Experiments in Art and Technology (E.A.T.) mounted the Pepsi Pavilion for the world's fair in Osaka, Japan. Contracted by the soft-drink behemoth to create a marketing spectacle for Expo 70, E.A.T. instead made something strange. They constructed an enormous spherical mirror dome that generated fully three-dimensional, inverted reflections—a stunningly surreal arena of real and virtual images, bodies, things, echoes, and lights. This was no mere specular mimesis. Rather, the pavilion pushed illusion into total simulation, into a realm of endless

replication that seemed to lose all connection to any original referent or ground.
Over the past decade, the technology–
and the dream–of a virtual world have
returned in full force. And if the headsets
still seem clunky, the engineering for
producing and viewing VR is undergoing
rapid new developments, portending a
near future in which fully immersive and
interactive virtual experiences are as
common as real ones. With 3D cameras
now filtering into art schools and studios
around the world, numerous artists have
worked on virtual reality and augmented
reality projects, including Pierre Huyghe,
Marina Abramović, Olafur Eliasson, and
Jeff Koons; younger artists such as Jon
Rafman, Sarah Meyohas, Jordan Wolfson,
and Rindon Johnson; and big-budget
Hollywood directors Alejandro Iñárritu
and Steven Soderbergh. We already live,
in many ways, in augmented reality–
where our phone screens, held out in front
of us, infiltrate our every gesture and move,
directing our way and changing our minds.
Whether artists can alter this adaptation–
stake out new ground, pose altogether
new realities–remains to be seen.

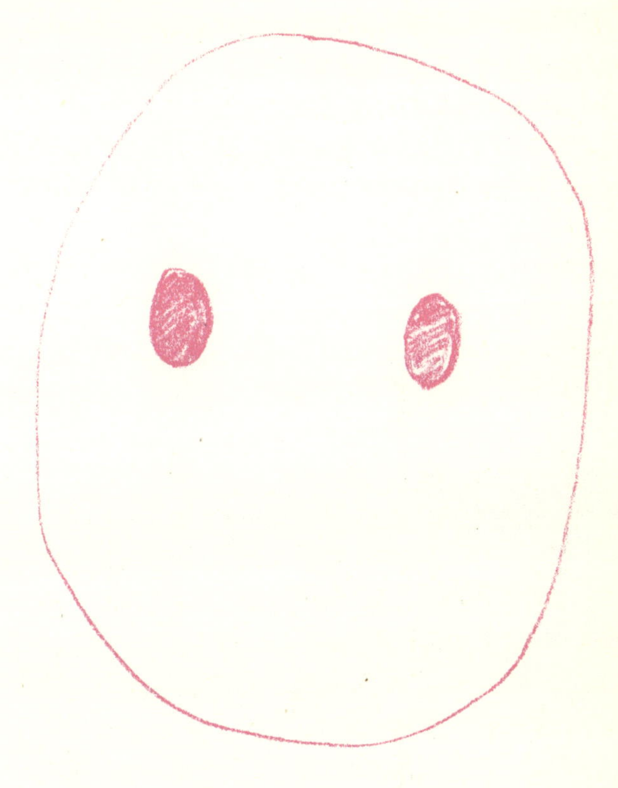

MOST EFFECTIVE AVATAR?
BELIEVABLE

Biofiction
Talk by
Anicka Yi

To enter virtuality you
need principles to change
the reality and turn
them over.

We are nonunpir to
the exlinutur of art

Korn

I've been thinking a lot about what

is natural, what is synthetic, and what
is post- or trans-natural vis-à-vis life.
Ostensibly, we've been changing
nature since the dawn of civilisation.
So it's important to unpack the conditions for knowing what we know—
the "how" and the "why" of what we
know with respect to the natural
versus synthetic.

For example, what is agriculture
if not bioengineering? Take, for example, mutations, which happen all the
time in nature. We are born from
mutations. Genes move laterally
between species, and so we can look
to a discipline like synthetic biology,
which is a young field growing with
momentum. It's an attempt at designing biology rather than just studying
it. It's related to genetic engineering,
and genetic engineering can lead to
transferring something like fish genes
into fruit so that we can make cold-
resistant fruit and have strawberries
in January. But that can also fall under
the framework of artificial intelligence
and digital technology, and the focus
of this Summit.

I'm specifically interested in the
ethical issues that synthetic biology
has raised about the origins of life, and

how the field is dismantling our thinking about evolution. Synthetic biologists think evolution is broken, error-prone, and difficult to decipher. And they call into question what constitutes a species in the first place. Transgenic technology is upending the traditional category of species. So, again, I have to ask, What is natural? How do we manage the ownership of life's materials? What responsibilities does designing biology carry, and should that design respond to the world and reflect its values—especially at a time when we can now see our own species' extinction on the horizon?

In 2015, I travelled to the Brazilian Amazon, which primarily drew me for its reputed vastness, its promise of innumerable biological specimens—in short, for the ineffable sublime. I went there to make a 3D video film that premiered at an exhibition in Kassel, curated by Susanne Pfeffer.

Like anybody else, I was interested in this mythology of the Amazon and what it means for humanism if everything can be connected, and no distinctions are made between human, organic, material, inanimate. But mostly I wanted to re-examine the boundaries that we have placed between the natural and the un-natural, and I felt that the Brazilian Amazon was a pretty good model to examine.

Again, we can look to synthetic biology, trans-naturalism, post-humanism, to think about multiple forms of consciousness like the cosmologies of indigenous peoples from the Amazon region. These groups follow a non-anthropocentric and non-hierarchical thinking about life, which is described by the influential Brazilian anthropologist, Eduardo Viveiros de Castro, whose work I was reading when I went on this trip and made this film. He coined the term *multi-natural perspectivism*, which takes into account that there are many different kinds of consciousnesses and that, maybe, we shouldn't have a hierarchical relationship where humans are on the top and other life forms are at the bottom.

For instance, in my film *The Flavor Genome*, nature is not conceived in absolute terms, but is assembled from a multitude of perspectives and perceptions. The film depicts a fluid mutation of species, at the same time showing how biology can no longer be separated from its narrative and its biography. To quote a line from the film, "Humanity still has not successfully metabolised the imperialist cultural pollution, the planetary despoliation, the vanished indigenous civilisations–key elements that comprise the flavour profile of the Tropics."

The film is an attempt to explore the Amazon, but also to ask how perceptions can be changed, how sensory experiences can allow for a different understanding of perception and consciousness. Taking these new sensory discoveries as its point of departure, *The Flavor Genome* imagines a chemical synthesis of plant and animal forms through an embodied cognition.

So far, I've been talking about animals and plants, but my work also embraces non-human persons by straddling synthetic biology and companion species. I look for the companionship of bacteria in our biota in order to emphasise the cyclical, the recursive, and the metabolic.

The view of living entities as co-subjective with us is gaining ground. We are entangled with objects–there are tens of thousands of species of bacteria in a given human's biota alone. We can think of theories of entanglement, as Karen Barad has elaborated, and the interconnectedness of all of us. Life is being reshuffled by fields like synthetic biology. Artists should play an important role in that reshuffling.

Bacteria are the workhorses of synthetic biology, which has been a collaborator subject in my work for the past few years now. Before I get into how I applied the bacteria, I just want to give a little context.

I've been adopting the term *biofiction* when talking about my work. It's a term coined by, Caroline Jones, a scholar at MIT, where I did a residency in 2015. Biofiction engages the mysterious cues in the relationship between biota and body, objects and subjects. It notes the fundamental strangeness of cellular self-assembly, that which confounds entropy by giving a common energy to living things and what has been stigmatised as pagan or savage. Biofiction, for me, means that which fuses the writing of life with the study of life, which also now includes an embrace of non-human persons.

Non-human persons is a concept used by indigenous people for whom all life is a person. So there can be a plant person, an animal person, a human person; every living thing has what the Hungarian bio-semiologist Jakob van Uexküll called an *umwelt,* a kind of self-centered world; and ostensibly a surrounding world beyond that.

Again, humans aren't exactly at the top of this hierarchy of life, and if we imbue a tick or a spider with the signals that might motivate her, she becomes a person with a world and a world-view; she is stimulated and perceived by a subject.

With that in mind, let's examine the materiality of this biofiction.

I made an exhibition in 2017 at the Guggenheim Museum in New York. For this show, I worked with a team of structural biologists, forensic chemists, and perfumers, as well as another artist to create an installation in which natural and technological forces appear as surging, unruly forms that are nonetheless clinically contained.

Visitors, at first encounter, saw an entryway or a kind of holding pen. The structure was related to the time I was preparing for the exhibition: at that moment, Donald Trump had just been elected and I was, like everyone else, very distraught, flummoxed, and I didn't really know how to respond in an art context. I didn't know what my role was in this state of crisis. Trump was threatening to implement a ban on Muslims entering the country—and, essentially, to kick people with Muslim backgrounds out of the country—and I think the entryway was a response, this crowded narrow corridor in which people would have to wait in order to enter the exhibition.

In the entrance, I also placed insect canisters, which emitted a scent. I've consistently sought to generate a sensory immersion that challenges the ocularcentric experience of art, and scent is a recurring component in my work. I use it sculpturally, linguistically, and to tap into memory, intangibility, synaesthesia, and a kind of presence through absence. When I activate smell, it's not a substitute—rather, it is an extension. I don't evoke scent where there is an absence of something to look at, but when I want to extend the senses, like rings of vision or olfactory experience, all triggers creating ellipses in consciousness. I want to examine our senses and how they're shaped through perception. Smell is pre-verbal, and yet we can take the real smell of something and combine its functionality with the stimulus of its smell and unlock semiotic codes. This is where biofiction can unfold. In this instance, as I've said, I got a little bit–I wouldn't say derailed, but it was a moment of pause. I had a different idea, and I went to a group of structural biologists at a laboratory in Columbia University in New York and I proposed a project. I asked them, "Can you help me create a drug–maybe even if it's fictional–a drug that would allow a human being to experience the perception of another living organism, like a coral reef, a pink dolphin, or another human being?" They humoured me for a while before they told me the inevitable–that it's biologically impossible to do so because, in order for me to experience the perception of a coral reef, I'd have to remould my brain to the brain of a coral reef or a pink dolphin, I would have to change all the neural networks, and we just don't have the technology to do that yet.

The way that I was able to move along with that narrative was that I decided to create a hybrid consciousness through olfaction–through chemical compounds. So I took sweat samples of Asian American females and a chemical analysis reading of some carpenter ants and I thought, if I can't literally experience the consciousness of a carpenter ant, perhaps if I combine their compounds together with the compounds emanating from the sweat of these human females, that would activate the biofiction.

The canisters in the entryway, then, are emitting this scent synthesized from the ants and the women, and the idea is that you would take it in, smell the fragrance, and, somehow, that would activate a biofictional drug and you would be endowed with the perception of this hybrid consciousness, hybrid organism.

It's commonly believed that humans have a poor sense of smell compared to other mammalian species. A lot of people come up to me and say, looking at my work, "I can't smell anything." I think that they're probably telling the truth, but it's kind of like playing the piano—you just have to practise it, and that's what perfume school is. You have to identify maybe a thousand different materials through your sense of smell and you will just, like playing an instrument, learn how to be more virtuosic with your instrument, your nose. I also think it's a kind of conditioning that we have adopted in most public spaces—especially in a place like New York—where we really, really, try not to smell anything at all, and there are legitimate reasons for that!

This idea of humans having a poor sense of smell derives not from empirical studies of human olfaction, but from a famous nineteenth-century anatomist's hypothesis that the evolution of human free will required a reduction in the proportional size of the brain's olfactory bulb. The human olfactory bulb is actually quite large in absolute terms and contains a similar number of neurons to that of other mammals. Moreover, humans have excellent olfactory abilities. We can detect and discriminate an extraordinary range of odours.

This ties into what I've been investigating in my work for the last couple of years and continue to do so about how the senses are conditioned socially. For example, the ocular is associated with the masculine because it represents discovery, knowledge, progress, and that's also a result of, maybe, a skewed idea of evolution. When humans got up off the ground and became erect bodies,

we started to privilege eyesight, whereas olfaction became associated with
that which was primitive, inscrutable,
mysterious, and entirely subjective.
And then, what would you call that?
You would ascribe that to the fem-
inine—which I reject.

I called the work at the beginning
of the Guggenheim show *Immigrant
Caucus*, riffing on its combination of
chemical compounds derived from
"alien" bodies: Asian American women
and carpenter ants. You walk in, you're
inoculated with this biofictional drug,
and you see this museological architecture of a diorama. The gallery's
central space features two opposing
dioramas, each providing a view into
a self-contained biosphere.

The first is lined with tiles that hold
a gelatinous substance called agar,
which is made of seaweed. I culti-
vated various strains of bacteria
sampled from sites within Manhattan's
Chinatown and Koreatown neighbour-
hoods. This living composition also
blooms across several sculptures,
as if an invasive life force has overrun
the environment—my sci-fi biofiction.

By using microbial materials,
I want to investigate the long-
standing paranoia around contagion

 On the one hand, I'm creating a living material representing the specific area of Manhattan in New York. You could even regard it as a portrait, if you will. But also, because bacteria can exist for hundreds of years–in a Verbier air duct, for example–I'm actually also incorporating history. But it's history crossed with metabolism and entropy, germinating a vast and violently bacteriological tableau.

The bacteria functions as a time-based work. The microbial sculpture renders visible the source of our unease–while foregrounding the politics and subjectivities of smell and touch and their impact on our empathic understanding of each other.

In other words, I think I am somebody who exists in the world; I respond to the world; I communicate in the world, and in New York. I think it was around 2014 that there was the big Ebola virus contagion freak-out paranoia, and nobody wanted to go into crowded spaces; nobody wanted to take the subway (I took the subway), no one wanted to touch the subway pole, and people were genuinely frightened because there were a couple of doctors who contracted the virus, and so the 24-hour-news cycle was inundated with the image of a nurse who was quarantined in a tent.

I wanted to make art that might address this palpable mood. I thought about contagion and the sense of hygiene and our discomfort around disease, and I thought that is really a formidable material to start working with. But also, when visiting an exhibition that contains a smell component or bacteria, you're not a passive visitor. There is a symbiotic relationship between the work and the visitor because you actually have to inhale the chemicals inside your orifices—through your nose and pores. In that sense, the person contributes to the biota tableau in the diorama.

Throughout the run of the exhibition, three months or so, the bacterial diorama started out with a few spores—a few blooms—and then progressively started to bloom all over. On a formal level, it was really interesting. It was a way of painting with a very uncooperative, unstable, unpredictable pigment and shading. It kept transforming.

Technically speaking, the entire structure was just a very, very sophisticated refrigeration unit. It was a kind of a walk-in refrigerator that I could enter from the back (only the biologists and I were allowed to handle the bacteria).

On the other side was a companion diorama that housed a colony of ants. Insects interest me because of their intricate division of labour and matriarchal social structure, as well as their sophisticated olfactory system, which guides their behaviour. The ants navigate a network of pathways that are reflected infinitely across mirrored surfaces evoking a massive data-processing unit in which their industrious movement embodies the flow of information.

The colony is exposed to the same hybrid scent that fills the corridor leading into the gallery, creating the possibility of a shared psychic expe-rience between ant and human. Ants in this way are also biopolitical agents, much like the bacteria are. I started with a pure fiction—a wish, and in a way, scent is also a wish and a fiction.

Annick Yi,
' As an artist I am
guided by the principle
or spirit of extinction.
Artists don't necessarily
think about forever. '

In response to my (Ann
Demeester) question whether
museums should not accept
the fundamental im-
permanence / ephemerality
of artworks produced now
instead of desperately
trying to conserve them
for eternity ?

Ann Demeester

VR, the Hottest Medium

Talk by Daniel Birnbaum & Douglas Coupland

WELL, ETHICS ~ MA

TRANSCRIPT OF TALK GIVEN IN VERBIER ON 19 JANUARY 2018

DB This conference is not only about virtual reality (VR). There are many kinds of new technologies that are based on new digital possibilities—augmented reality, mixed reality, new kinds of holograms, maybe. Do you think virtual reality will radically change our lives?

DC Yes—and an unqualified "yes"! I think anything that allows you to escape from yourself, whether it's drugs or alcohol or opiates or broadcast television, we're always going to want that.

Let me tell you about the first experience I had with virtual reality. It was in my living room in Vancouver, where I live, and we had some good friends over, and it was this beautiful July afternoon, and the light was coming through the leaves on the tree… It was just a gorgeous, perfect, perfect day in my favourite room on Earth, and there was this friend that works at Mozilla down in the Bay Area, and he brought up the most recent version of Oculus, and I'd never used one before, and so I put it on, and suddenly I was floating above a purple swamp in Louisiana, and there were lights off in the distance—so I chased the lights like that *[slightly rocking from side to side*

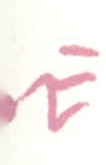

in his chair]—a very, very simple experience, and then, "Let's do another." It was asteroid mining on Jupiter or Saturn or something, except you could only look. You couldn't really put your hands in or do anything—so, altogether it was maybe three and a half minutes, and then I took the goggles off and I looked at the real world and I thought, "What a dump this place is!" And I realised, "Oh, my God! This thing is going to win; there's no way it cannot win."

The only caveat of VR experience is that if you stop suddenly or if you cut scenes, then it really affects your vestibular system and you feel seasick or you will puke—but there's also this thing called "VR sadness." which is what I experienced. People put these things on and they come out, and they never quite return to the full world, and a part of them is invested in this machine.

DB So it's an escapist kind of technology. It will help us like drugs or alcohol. Is it a negative thing, you think?

DC Well, it's going to happen. I mean, VR is this asteroid that's going to hit the planet, apparently, in 2023. I mean, if I really had my act together, I'd be out there making a VR slasher movie or VR pornography or VR gaming or something. It's going to happen. There's going to be a first VR porno, there's going to be a first VR slasher film. So what are you going to do? You can't fight it. You try to understand it. Have you tried it yet?

DB I have tried it a little bit.

DC What was your experience?

DM Yup. I was similarly… Not shocked. That's not the right word, and I didn't see wonderful things, but I looked at it at the Warner Brothers studio in London.

DC Like cartoons?

DB They were cartoons, but I don't really know what they were. I think Disney Productions or something, but it was, you know, you turn around and there's a very large gorilla there, but like really large, and there's a snake which is *that* close, and it's *super*-naturalistic. And these are, I presume, children productions–so, what is going to happen to children?! If you grow up with that as a normal kind of entertainment, not a little cartoon or a little book or something that we grew up with, but with hyper-realistic jungle scenes with crazy mega-gorillas one millimetre away from you, you will grow up with a strange kind of understanding of what's normal.

DC Oh, you would, wouldn't you? I was saying yesterday that in the 1960s, when hippies just suddenly appeared on the scene around '65, everyone was like, "Who are these people? Where do they come from?", and we realised they came from television, and now we have millennials, and they're coming out of the early Internet era, and then you are going to have these next post-millennial (maybe one and a half generations from now) who won't even really have a connection with the physical world, I don't think, and then–is it a bad thing? Maybe it's just an evolutionary stage.
DB But even if the effects are stronger, the wish to leave this world, isn't that basically what art and literature and theatre and cinema, all of this, is about? I mean, didn't Hieronymus Bosch and Salvador Dalí take some heavy kind of stuff? Isn't that just the same thing?
DC I think it's actually a religious impulse to want to exit the body. I mean, earlier I was upstairs in the lounge looking at my iPhone. You know, thirty years ago, I would have been reading poems by Rilke. So, something's changed there.

DB But you can read Rilke on your iPhone.

DC It's not the same. In terms of the escapist need, it's something everyone wants to do. Maybe we should figure out why it is that we want to escape.

DB So you think VR is a medium that is somehow stronger than others, and that will more or less dominate or kill all other media?

DC Completely—it just overtakes your body; you're captured by it. It taps into the reptile part of your brain as well as the frontal cortex and all your gravity systems. You know, when the doorbell rings and you are in VR, you are not going to be able to answer the door or something like that *[stretching out his hand to turn a handle]*. You're really absolutely inside it; you're completely within it.

DB I forgot to mention that Douglas is not only an author and a cultural critic and many things, he's also an artist and designer, *plus*—importantly here, perhaps—you wrote a very interesting book on Marshall McLuhan! Now I remember that, as part of that, that was an easy way in for me, somehow, since I know so little about these things that I could ask questions that somehow relate to McLuhan because, I did know a little bit about him, and he distinguishes between what he calls "hot" and "cold" mediums. What is that, again? And what is VR?

DC First of all, the "hot"/"cold" thing, even after all these years, I don't quite get it. But I'd say VR is probably the hottest medium there is.

DB Because it absorbs you totally?

DC Completely. There is nothing else you can do. You know, a lot of younger people don't know who McLuhan is or, if they do, they only have a very faint idea. He was this English teacher in Toronto in the early 1960s who, at the age of fifty, began discussing changes that are happening inside our minds, bodies, and societies; and, through a chain of really, weirdly, unrelatable expe-riences, he was able to, basically, see the Internet fifty years before it happened, but he didn't know the correct interfaces–so, if you reread him now, he'll be using Yeats or pamphleteers from the eighteenth century to describe what's basically PayPal, or CNN. I'm continuing to read him, because he's not correct just up to 2018, Daniel, he's probably going to go way further into the future, and I think that if I continue to research him, we'll probably find out more about what VR is going to do to us.

DB If virtual reality is going to change our lives, it will also change a sub-category—small, but very important for some of us: namely, art—and what do you think? I mean, now there are people here in the room who are working with this, but do you think it's an entirely new art form coming? Or will it duplicate everything that has already been done, and recreate it in VR?

DC Well, the sensory part of it is so overwhelming and so wonderful that you forget that they're probably going to have to throw some storylines in there too, and have new fables. Probably what Netflix is to TV, this is going to be the next Netflix, perhaps, but even then a bit more saturated, a bit more intense. It is the future of narrative. I'm certainly looking at it and going, "Ok, what story can you tell here that you can't tell anywhere else?" I think that probably this could be a lot about James Cameron and with the movies he makes with people who are blue, what was that again?

DB *Avatar*.

DC I think that's the first direction, maybe, with a very big budget.
DB I know that Tate did something now to accompany their Modigliani show. That's a vehicle, a way to make people know about their show, and people can watch it even if they don't go to the museum, but art that is produced *for*, or *in*, or with this new medium has also started—at the Whitney Biennial, at the last Venice Biennale. It has many problems of a practical nature. You know, we could show something here because we're a hundred people or something, but with the big museums or biennales and stuff where there are hundreds of thousands, it's very difficult, but there is something also with it that I wonder about.

I think we talked about this—but there's something a little bit autistic, solipsistic, isolated, about it. You know, you put on that thing, and friends leave—are gone—and you feel you're great out there on Jupiter, but I mean, when you go to art shows, isn't it fun to actually go with someone? I would love to walk through a museum with you and talk to you whilst looking at paintings, and this seems…
DC Yeah. People just look strange

when they're wearing those goggles–
there is no way around it–and, whoever is designing them, that is the
golden design ring of the next twenty
years. They have to look like you're
not being cocooned by a superior
species, is what they ought to look like.
DB You're a designer–so…
DC But maybe there is a way. I've
got them on; you've got them on;
and we can actually go in a space
together, and I think the new Steven
Spielberg movie, *Ready Player One*,
is about just that.

I mean, if that was an app, like go
through the Moderna Museet with
Daniel Birnbaum, that would be kind
of wonderful, actually. So, maybe
we're projecting isolation into a
situation that could actually be very
rich in shared experience.
DB Of course, reading a novel is
also a lonesome thing.

You sit there and you read your
book, and you're alone.
DC Maybe books are overrated.
DB *[Chuckles]*
DC Yes, I just said that! On live
streaming on international whatever.
DB *[Laughing]*
DC Well, maybe books were just a
necessary interim technology that

had to happen in order to get us to VR, and now we can get rid of our books. *[Stunned silence.]*
DB Yeah…
DC Your brains are dribbling…
DB Yes, I don't know what to say to that exactly. But, beyond them being ugly, because I agree, it's very unattractive, this whole technology. They look silly, and you're looking stupid, and people look like clowns when they're wearing them, but that might change, I presume, that they will look like Ray-Bans or I don't know what.
DC They'll figure it out. There's that photo, I think, most people have seen now of a commuter railway car going from the suburbs of London into the city, and every single guy (there are no women in it) is reading the same paper all at once. So there you have another example of isolation within a crowd. If they're all reading the same stories then, maybe, they're basically wearing goggles together. I mean, people don't change, I don't think. They just take the same old behaviours and re-inflect them in new ways.

So, I do think that the aspect of VR that is being overlooked is the

and I think that's going to be quite wonderful, and I really, really look forward to that.
DB Are you going to do things in VR?
DC I don't know. By 2023 I might be retired in Arizona chasing waterfalls in my Tesla or something.

I would like to, though. Unless you can get your hands in there, it's not going to be a very satisfying experience, but I think they're working on that already, right? See, it's going to happen. Maybe we should start at the studio. How difficult is it? Is it crazy difficult to film something and have it translated into the goggles?
DB It's moving very quickly, I presume. But, I'm not sure I understood what you said about the fact that at the museum we walk through and you're two or three people. In virtual reality one *can* share a space – of course…
DC It's like you're doing a Google doc or something. You can work on it together.
DB But then I see you as an avatar…
DC: Well, my avatar would definitely be in there–not me. Yeah.
DB So it doesn't have to be a kind of a lonesome…

DC No, it's not about isolation. You can investigate a space with someone in Antarctica if you're set-up properly. It's just that it looks so strange. I think it was Pink Floyd, or was it Led Zeppelin–they did this album cover designed by Hipgnosis studios back in the early '70s, and they took '50s stock photos of families or people in their car or whatever, and they put this black object in it, and it was *insanely* prescient. You'd have this family, and everyone was just sort of staring at this black thing, and I always wondered what it was. Of course, it ended up being these things we live with.

I think that things stop being weird very, very quickly. Do you remember when *google* sounded like a stupid word to say, and now it's just a word? There is going to be a very awkward stage at the beginning, and I think there is going to be a sort of Bitcoin stage to it as well, as everyone tries to jump in and cash in as quickly as they can.

DB I would say, the moment when it becomes a normal thing–a kind of every-day device–is, I guess, the moment when it's totally wireless and also in your phone, I guess, and you just have it there, and the glasses look like Ray-Bans or something else. Otherwise, if you have to go to a special place, put on some ugly goggles with a huge computer, that's not so attractive, but it all happens quickly now.

DC I know what you're saying…

DB If you could just wish for something – what would it be?

DC Ok, back in the '60s–like, "Wow! We have technology! We've got some artists. Why don't you guys make art out of it?" And there's a certain optimism about it, like conquering a new continent, and now everyone looks at these machines like, "How can I make money out of this?", or "How do I make it pay off?" There doesn't seem to be the same will to make art out of it yet, and it might be just because the interface is so clunky. It's obviously going to happen.

DB Hasn't the dominant trend in the art world been to be sceptical of technology, that it is something scary? But there are moments when that's not the case. I remember we were both in a conference about "Les Immatériaux," the exhibition curated by Jean-François Lyotard, that had utopian, techno-optimistic tendencies. They had both, and there are movements such as E.A.T. and the group in Germany, Zero, and way back in the early twentieth century we had Futurism, which was, maybe, naïvely optimistic about war machines and military technology.

DC There is Kraftwerk.

DB Yeah. In the art world at least, and you're partly in the art world–you're in many worlds–but people have been a little bit, you know, traumatised by technology. That it is more a problem and a dangerous thing rather than a possibility.

DC Well, around 2029 the VR equivalent of the bicycle wheel on a chair is going to happen. That's the exciting part–wondering what it's going to be. We're going to find out. I don't know!

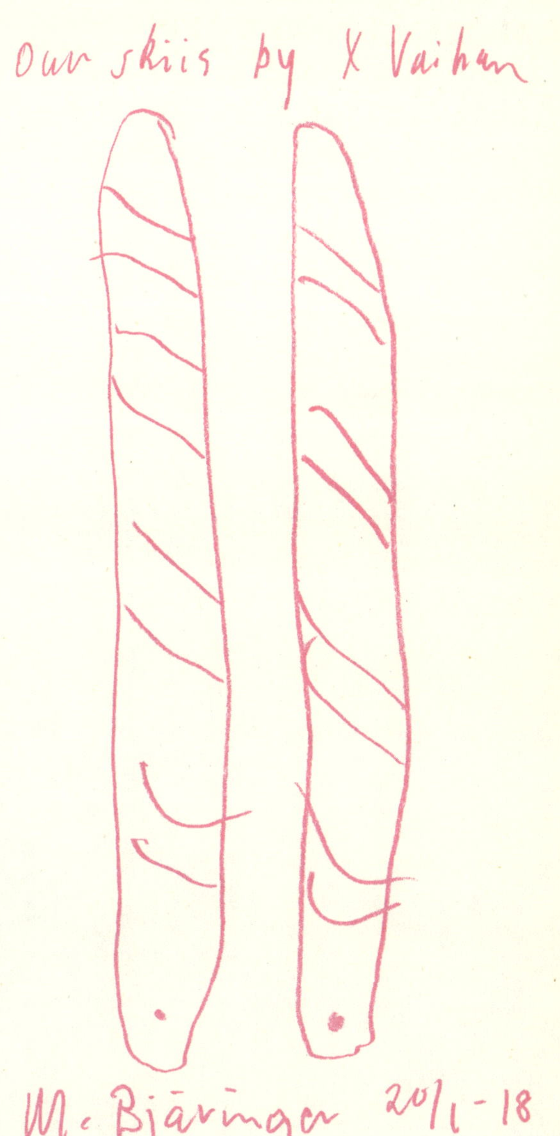
Our skiis by X Vaihan
Mr. Bjäringer 20/1–18

Douglas Coupland

MORE THAN REAL

DINNER PARTIES
WERE MORE FUN
WHEN YOU
COULD LIE

WHAT IS THE DATA EQUIVALENT OF PERSPECTIVE?

YOU
AND YOUR
SELFIE
ARE
MERGING

KNOWING EVERYTHING TURNS OUT TO BE SLIGHTLY BORING

I AGREE
TO THE ABOVE
TERMS
AND
CONDITIONS

THE CLOUD WILL ALLOW YOU TO SPEAK WITH YOURSELF

I WOULD
LIKE TO
SPEAK
WITH A
HUMAN BEING
PLEASE

DISCUSSING THE FUTURE MEANS YOU BLINDLY ENDORSE IT

I MISS
MY
PRE-INTERNET
BRAIN

I HATE TALKING ON THE PHONE THESE DAYS BUT I DON'T KNOW WHY

MACHINES ARE TALKING ABOUT YOU AND ME BEHIND OUR BACKS

'Losslessness'
Ed Atkins

BEAUFUL CHA

A scene from a recent video work, 'Good Smoke', plays throughout: an empty cell, windowless save for a huge circular hole in the right hand wall; an upright piano on the left; flickering fluorescent tubes hang from the ceiling; theatrical smoke circulates; a distant wind. Once the talk has finished, a boy dressed in Elizabethan costume—ruffs, brocaded purple jerkin, curling leather shoes—dives through the hole into the room. He rolls and staggers to his feet, woozily crosses to the piano, sits, and begins to play a loop of Jürg Frey's 'Extended Circular Music #2', weeping all the while.

I'd like to talk about loss in relation to the digital, and in particular the digital moving image. In this brief talk, different kinds of loss will get confused: psychological, corporeal, the deliberately spurned, unknowably gone. Loss will be apprehended both literally and figuratively, oftentimes in a welter of the two. I'm going to lean most heavily on a psychoanalytic figuration and a mortal, existential literalism of loss: two of the limits of loss's sense and affect. In talking through some of this, I hope to sketch a particular kind of ethics of literality and figuration, with emphasis on how these two modes are at work in the digital moving image. I should say that loss, here, should be understood in the possessive. As in, all of what follows should be inscrutably caveated by autobiography.

The title of this talk is 'Losslessness', loss's cybernetically bred correlative. Losslessness, in all its clunkily appended vernacular, refers to a category of data compression algorithm that allows original data to be perfectly reproduced. 'Losslessness', part abstracted, implicitly invites a mistaking of technology's progression for a fantasy of immortality; built-in obsolescence is prosaically confused with death: loss proper. Losslessness explicitly pertains to a limitlessness regarding the possible reproducibility of a thing, but it also speculates an end to loss as a precondition of everything. 'Speculates', because losslessness is conjectural and hyperbolic–a re-labelling of loss. Empirically, losslessness, as some kind of paradoxically caveated annexation, is itself always already lost to experience; it is simply another category of loss. Literal empiricism, however, is an ever more rarified position. Contemporary digital reproductions' persistent demonstration of a lossless material promise sufficiently ironises loss's hegemony over The Inevitable (and over experience's veracity). Particularly when reality's already dubious actuality has become so fantastically subtended by the digital: enough to shift loss's proximity to material personal experience. Loss, felt, gets repressed at a clip equivalent to the refresh rate of an infinite reproduction, dissembling loss through its immortal figuration, and with it, those things that might previously have been mourned in their loss.

'Loss', in the technological, specifically digital sense, has all but shrugged off its physical, etymological forbears. Like 'rendering', 'capturing', 'processing', etc., 'loss' is a negative effect of a now welcome, obsoleted failure of tech. 'Losslessness' is a solution to a problem concocted inside the language and its particular tech semiology; a kind of problem modelled, coolly, according to some successional capitalistic paradigm, rendered a weird sort of natural, a kind of evolution-as-in-built-

obsoletism. A disinterested suspension, as-if of insuperable nature, apart.
Such disinterest steeps seeming
technological straightforwardness,
too, saturating not just its lexicons
but also our presumption of the innate-
ness of its processes. It's a sleight that
conflates capitalism's waveform of
progress and dissimulates certain
desires and meanings behind plan-
ned obsolescence, differentiated from,
say, the evolution of Galapagos finches away from whatever Galapagos
finches were before they were
Galapagos finches. Insofar as it sticks
evolutionary process with the motives
of design, tech's natural world has a
distinctly creationist hue, a tack that
could be the M.O. of certain consumer
products: user-friendliness more often
than not pervades in order to maintain
ignorance, and is engaged in econo-
mically justified mollification. The kind
of capitulation that a spiritualistic natural world might apparently ethically
urge, needs either some sort of heu-
ristic detachment, or otherwise a
comfortingly justifiable disregard
of material and mortal experiences
and consequence. Experiences
and consequences of loss, in
our example.

In a so-called natural order of things, technology is in thrall to other, larger, celestial movements. This means that, left uninterrupted, in due course technology is liable to be straightforwardly disposed of, according to the logic of whatever capitalistic progress, at the altar of obsolescence and its erroneous determination as natural and the apparent Way Things Are. On these terms, mortality confers only the loss of value and timely replacement. Mortality, here, is a pejorative. Or a violence allegorised, even as it burlesques the truly mortal by pertaining to inevitability. This violence divests mortality of a great slew of attendant undertakings: care, mourning, intimacy, affective recognition– all of which are in direct correspondence with mortality, but only if mortality is understood as ontological. Only if mortality is a condition of life rather than of economic process–and only if understood literally rather than figuratively.

The relationship between the literal and the figurative is fraught; a given literal meaning is more often than not in disagreement–if not political conflict–with the figurative meaning. This paradox is rehearsed at every stage of the stuff I make and, I would argue, is at the heart of my practice's attempt at a document: its attempt to encounter and afford the paradoxes of its seeming contingencies in order to better propose how it might break or resolve certain misplaced ironies and dissimulations, in turn to affirm a kind of caring application of the literal and the figurative.

In the videos I make, I want to make conspicuous my attachment to the vicissitudes of the technologies that describe the work's limits—to make conspicuous the necessity of any technologically-incumbent artist's attachment to the vicissitudes of their chosen medium. An artist's first approach to some glistening new tech will more often than not be to cleave to the edge of the tech, to trace its perimeter in order to *figure* whatever aspect ratios or resolutions and all the other hindering apparatuses of apparent A/V fidelity as *literal*. This for the purposes of exposition, initially, and for the particular elucidatory pleasures of finitude, latterly. In so doing, an artist might be seen to be *incorporating* the tech. As in, making it corporeal, analogue, mortal. Moving toward the world, with a Freudian lope, sadistically–preemptively: the subject/object relation seemingly built entirely around sadism's hegemony as ur-relation, a presumed preventative feint, just to be sure.

This literality is a rebuttal of the desires of the tech–its apparent correct usage and, at the other end, its specialist unpacking. The artist's relationship to the *use* of a piece of technology whose complexity makes its parameters far more restricted than, say, a pencil is to reject the very idea of use. And because so many of the desires of a technology relate to upholding its inconspicuousness, one of the first things an artist might do when wielding it, would be to retrieve the technology from whatever quagmire of figuration in which it had sequestered itself. Whether that figurative hiding place is representational verisimilitude or, similarly, disappearance from the field of view by extreme intimacy or extimacy to its user–the technology constantly seeks to be lost.

The consumer-grade portion of tech finds some figured endophytic relation to its user, whereas the specialist piece of kit is figured alien–almost state-level alien, like the military or industry or space or whatever other intangible. It is, perhaps, hyper-objectivised–pushed to a point of irretrievable unwieldiness. The exponential growth of these relations is cybernetics proper, even if, for me, it's perhaps more appositely considered through the mutable lens of psychoanalysis. To reiterate and to be clear: loss is our exemplar. Both those poles of proximity (consumer/ specialist) vanish the tech to the general populous. Certainly to ideological ends, but also for more convoluted reasons, as regards any consequential relation. As in, the tech's vanishing is part of a maintenance of a fantasy of holism, coherency. Or perhaps the loss of the tech obtains the seeming maintenance of the ego and the ego's correctly deluded place, hierarchically speaking.

'Correct usage', as regards a piece of technology, is a pragmatic normality that bleeds out into ideology, social determinism, and so on. So the artist must first set out to *find* the technology. Or rather, the artist must first understand the technology as lost. This *finding* is cast metaphorically, although there is, relatively speaking, a movement toward the literal in this retrieval. If unacknowledged absence is the precondition of technology's successful ebb, then the figurative act of finding is, at least, a literal act of making *present*. In this account, technology proper is always already lost, and by disingenuous design. Ignorance is a kind of pall to appease guilt. So the subject bypasses the need for the object by regarding it as a loss beyond the reach of the self: the subterranean ground of the teach—its reality—is apparently beyond impactful range. The loss is never understood, simply repressed. Insofar as the lost object becomes internalised through its dissimulation, the relationship is neurotic, according to Freudian psychoanalysis.

In most cases, where the ethics of corporate industry, factory conditions, state violence, environmental horror, political dogma, etc., are known (and this, really, is most of the time—or at least suspected *all* of the time), the consciously oblivious loss of technology is entirely desirable in order to repress the trauma of the technology's fact. This kind of imperative repression—imperative in order to function coherently, according to all kinds of vast, contractual mores—creates a kind of aimless melancholy or shame. An awful, disinterested shrug laps the melancholic. In contrast, acknowledging the lost object sets in motion a shift from melancholy to purposive mourning. By example, acknowledging the bodies traumatised in coltan mines and sweatshops retrieves those bodies, allows the possibility of mourning them, of witnessing their loss.

More prosaically, sufficiently acknowledging that the movies are constituted by a procession of lifelessness—that the moving image is an illusion—*finds* simultaneously those intestinal coils of celluloid, and the ideological engine behind that illusion. Mourning might best be thought of as a way of properly tracking and acknowledging loss: whether in death or knowledge or empathy or truth. Suddenly the camera is visible in the mirror. The VHS tracking remains permanently, deliberately unresolved, becomes rhythmic. Music and foley buzz and keel, then abruptly cut. The world and its representation are distinguished, immanence evades narration. Melancholia transmutes into mourning and the real work can begin.

Literality can only be a functionary of recouping the mortal when such recoupment relates to matter. Structuralist approaches to the moving image understand a difference between effect and reality. By uncovering the workings, whether celluloid or shutter, one analogises the 'uncovering' of other realities. One repudiates illusions of all kinds by repudiating the illusion of the moving image. Making literal, here, flows into the figurative, while analogy or metaphor must appear in order for the act to *mean* beyond whatever microcosm. The process is parabolic, requiring significant relation between, say, persistence of vision and propaganda. Fundamentally, both structuralist and deconstructive methods require that there be a thing of whose structure it is possible to expose. It subsequently requires that the illusion either remain or be put back in place, to allow sufficient function to sustain critique. And, really, a particular order of movement between literal and figurative is necessary for structural analyses to function.

Clearly, this pertains to the mortal analogue above, insofar as uncovering the workings of the living body means violence, or can better be described via abjection. As regards the moving image, illusion is a condition of its being: a suspension of disbelief is a condition of its encounter, even if that suspension of disbelief is in turn suspended by the insistence of its partial dismantling for the sake of structural comprehension. In other words, the simultaneous and continued functioning of structure *with* its surface, whilst they are simultaneously observed, is essential to the reading. Like understanding how a cat works by observing its innards, while it continues to *work*, engine purring. If retrieving the lost object of a moving image technology lies in exposing its material reality as well as the lives, processes, and politics that flow into a materiality deferred by the illusion that defines the medium, then acknowledging it is made possible by structural revelation simultaneous to continued function. Critically, this happens in a movement that is more or less against the desires of that technology. Insofar as this process is political, it also abounds with agency: deconstructing the object confers the freedom of the subject.

And again, the literal is asserted in order to re-found figuration.

Figural to literal to figural: the lost object is acknowledged as lost in order to counter the neurotic consequences of repression, and to begin a reparative move from melancholia to mourning. Mourning is mantric, inasmuch as it involves the naming of an object through the description of its absence, while literalisation is equivalent to death. Both *find* their subject, retrieve them from the disbelief of a life, of figuration, while affirming the absence of the very thing whose finitude they affirm. Literalisation renders loss, rather than the thing that was lost. Literalisation describes the figurative as such: it delimits its existence by divulging its immanence.

The literal is the end of language. And all of this is profoundly complicated by the digital. If technology's implicit desire is to disappear by a movement of natural progress, the digital pushes that figurative idea towards the literal. The digital cusps both figuration and the literal, unmooring both, disrupting the ways in which the two might move between one another, be recognisable as one rather than the other. Digital technologies seem so fiercely figured, and so wholly welcomed and afforded as a kind of ethical relief, the combination of which is surely most conspicuously capable of eroding the capacity to tell the difference between what is and what is not. Or, more opaquely, what is and what is also, with that 'also' a fine print of terms and conditions to unspool in great, abject reports from far away and next door; to be scrolled blithely through in order to reach the 'I agree' checkbox. A confusion of literality and figuration means that 'the cloud' remains a cloud, literally, while also operating as an image of a cloud—the one obliterates the conditions of the other, sending clouds, along with whatever acceded personal details, to some weird no-place of fug and ignorance and clouds, literally. The digital does not have literal analogues. To return to mourning and melancholia, the digital represses its lost object by literal figuration, and those neurotic symptoms that riddle the melancholic become a condition of the digital. Somewhere over there, countless acres of bunkered server farms wolf inestimable amounts of energy, overheating and strobing and storing and producing illusions playing out thousands of miles away, out of sight and out of mind.

The melancholia suffuses and neurotic tics of shame and guilt play across faces quieted by an ignorance advanced by those impossible, labyrinthine convolutions that constitute digital figuration and its disappeared, literal structure. Losslessness abounds and the mourning made possible by naming it–by affirming it in order to process it–is made figurative, literally.

Writing this, I'm struck by the queasy clarity of my own neuroses–as well as their positive motility: how I've almost always wanted my videos firstly to be analogous to people, to bodies, to experience, to loss. For my videos to stand as a kind of metaphysical surrogate for what I long for, the finite holism of a person's existence. For years I rehearsed the idea that the videos I was making were dead men, albeit figuratively speaking. Descended, psychically, from that literal dead man who began this whole sorry mess for me. Making videos became about reparative mourning, though not therapy, per se–extending outwards from mourning's most literal, funereal wellspring, to address a whole host of melancholic, neurotic attachments–transposing them into aspects of my life possible to be understood, if never, importantly, *got* (there is nothing of applicable use or value, here, at the wake). Most importantly, mourning intuits the moving image in a way that felt like forcible congruence at first, but which has expanded to encounter the structure of the medium, its affective modes, its burlesque of substance dualism–its striving for representational cogency. Immanence asserts the loop of every video I make, circumscribes fidelity and stands against lossnessness. Loss is the sublime condition of any experience.

A LARGE PORTION OF THIS TEXT WAS ORIGINALLY WRITTEN TO ACCOMPANY THE EXHIBITION 'GENERATION LOSS: 10 YEARS OF THE JULIA STOSCHEK COLLECTION', DÜSSELDORF, 2017–18.

Information wants to be expensive

Caring for Time-Based Media in Major Museums

Karen Archey

WILL MACHINES EVER DO
WE ALL SECRETLY HOPE
WILL NOT !

Artists have often used the mass-produced technologies of their era, whether to comment on the urgencies of their historical moment or reflect on more universal or philosophical topics. The recent history of time-based media dates back to the 1960s, when technologies such as video cameras and televisions became affordable to the common consumer. Artists such as Nam June Paik explored the subject of television through the materiality of the television set, which was increasingly present in middle-class homes. Vito Acconci, Joan Jonas, Bruce Nauman, and others experimented with film and video camera technologies, and traversed the shift from celluloid film to magnetic tape-based video capture in the 1970s. Later, in the 1980s, Dara Birnbaum challenged the corporatization of broadcast television and its control over public consciousness. In the 1990s, as desktop computers became widespread, artists began to make use of the internet as a medium. Dutch artist collective JODI, for example, became known for hiding a diagram of a bomb within the source code of their homepage—suggesting something foul afoot within the very structure of the web. Over the next decades, as the internet gave rise to the social media of Web 2.0, artists took to social networking websites such as YouTube and Instagram. Artist Ann Hirsch posed as a narcissistic teen vlogger in the late naughts, and in 2010 the duo Eva and Franco Mattes controversially staged a suicide on the video chat platform ChatRoulette. Today, discussions such as the 2018 Verbier Art Summit are dominated by talk of two relatively new technologies currently most hyped by the tech sector and investment markets alike: virtual reality and artificial intelligence. Artists such as Jeff Koons, Marina Abramović, Olafur Eliasson, Jordan Wolfson, and Jon Rafman currently use virtual reality to explore notions of world-building within their work, while artists such as Lynn Hershman Leeson, Trevor Paglen, and Harm van den Dorpel have experimented with artificial intelligence and machine learning.

The only continuous thread uniting the incredibly wide breadth of topics touched on by the aforementioned artists is their use of technology—and, particularly, its continuous and pressing obsolescence. These works are dependent on mass-produced technology, which is often no longer available or reproducible mere decades after the artworks' creation. For example, how is one to replace a Nam June Paik monitor in 2018, when 1960s television sets have been out of production for fifty years? As artists and art professionals, how do we keep these important works alive for future generations to experience? Further, how do we contextualize the experience of past technology for our current day? This essay examines the acquisition, display, and conservation practices related to time-based media works, outlining the nascent practices of the institution where I work, the Stedelijk Museum Amsterdam, comparing these strategies with those of other large-scale museums with considerable holdings in time-based media.

It's a complicated business: technological obsolescence is the most urgent factor in time-based media conservation, and many museums throughout the world have developed specialized methods to strategize the display, acquisition, and preservation of time-based art. Each of these institutions organizes its exhibition and conservation responsibilities in a different way, and time-based media are rarely lumped into one categorization. Thus performance, video, and media curators are generally structured as separate roles. For example, at the Whitney Museum of American Art, individual curators are assigned to the collection concentrations performance, film/video, photography, etc. At the Museum of Modern Art, New York, performance and media fall under one department while film falls under another. Similarly, Tate Modern in London separates performance and film into two departments. At Tate, their content frequently overlaps due to the entwined history of performance, film, and video in the late 1960s and '70s.

At the Stedelijk Museum Amsterdam, where I am Curator of Contemporary Art, Time-based Media, I work with all time-based mediums, as my title would suggest. I organize exhibitions as well as the performance program, and develop a conservation department for time-based media. My first assignments were solo exhibitions by Dutch photographer

Rineke Dijkstra, American composer and artist Stefan Tcherepnin, and Swedish mathematician and sound artist Catherine Christer Hennix, though her exhibition primarily comprised painting. The director who hired me, Beatrix Ruf, envisioned the Stedelijk to be a "post-medium" institution, and she and the Chief Curator Bart van der Heide have assigned exhibitions as such: the time-based media curator can curate a photography show, and the photography curator can curate a painting show (my colleague, Stedelijk photography curator Hripsimé Visser is organizing an exhibition of German painter Gunther Förg as I write this essay). This formation echoes that of the Whitney, where curators who specialize in one medium's concentration can organize an exhibition with works in another medium: for example, former Whitney performance curator Jay Sanders organized a large-scale Alexander Calder exhibition in 2017. This "post-medium" position acknowledges how artists themselves have taken complex positions regarding medium-based practices in recent decades. Very seldom do artists work in only one

    CARING FOR TIME-BASED MEDIA IN MAJOR MUSEUMS

medium throughout their entire oeuvre; rather, their exploration of content often extends to many mediums of varying levels of familiarity to the artist.

Yet how can an institution truly embody such a "post-medium" position when it has hundreds or thousands of objects to preserve, the care of which is dependent on its medium? For pragmatic purposes relating to collection care, curators must persist in their medium-specific collection work, particularly for time-based media, which often require unusually fast-paced upkeep lest they become obsolete. A conservator must regularly check, and ideally show, media-based works in order to assess impending issues such as hardware or software failure; sometimes things just flat-out break. The display, acquisition, and preservation of time-based media are thus intimately intertwined.

At the Stedelijk, I am responsible for the intake and care of all time-based media works. These mediums include video, new media such as internet art and software-based art, sound, performance and choreography-based works, slides, and film. As I began my position in early 2017, the Stedelijk had just completed its first joint acquisition of a suite of digital artworks, spurred by the closure of neighboring Museum of the Image (MOTI) in Breda, Netherlands. This museum dedicated to time-based media was forced by the municipality of Breda to merge with Stedelijk Museum Breda. Yet MOTI had budget for acquisitions for the year of 2016 and thus proposed to the Stedelijk—better known as a contemporary art institution rather than a state museum, as is Stedelijk Museum Breda—to jointly acquire works for both collections, assuring their longevity. Totaling seventeen works, this acquisition comprised well-known internet artists such as Olia Lialina, Petra Cortright, and Vuk Cosić, and particularly prioritized renowned internet artists with a connection to the Netherlands, including Martine Neddam (Mouchette.org), Rafael Rozendaal Jan Robert Leegte, and Constant Dullaart. My first months at the Stedelijk consisted of assessing what the collection comprises, its needs, and how the time-based media department is structured in comparison with those of other large-scale

     CARING FOR TIME-BASED MEDIA IN MAJOR MUSEUMS

museums. Ward Janssen, who primarily compiled the suite of works jointly acquired by MOTI and the Stedelijk, stayed on to help "hand the torch" in order to properly take in and begin researching these important works.

The time-based media department at the Stedelijk is now an unofficial interdepartmental working group consisting of myself, a registrar, an archivist, and, most importantly, the museum's media conservator Gert Hoogeveen–whose actual title is Coordinator of Audiovisual Art Handling. The fact that Gert technically works in the AV department means that his responsibilities are primarily exhibition-related rather than connected to conservation. Conversely, at Tate Modern, conservation and exhibition responsibilities are completely separated. This has its advantages and disadvantages: more time is spent on the individual concerns of caring for and displaying time-based media works, but sometimes this division in labor creates a gap in knowledge when different parties store and install works. In practice, Gert manages the AV department and acts as a living record of everything related to time-based media at the Stedelijk, while carving out time to work on conservation projects. Currently, the Stedelijk is transitioning away from solely relying on the external media preservation organization LIMA for its video and media conservation, toward a new structure in which the museum creates a working group with specialists from various departments. As Gert is retiring in 2020, the museum is preparing for his departure with a restructuring of his responsibilities. The profile of Gert's replacement, and which department they will work in, is yet to be determined.

Like many institutions, the Stedelijk's conservation department is object-based in nature: Gert likes to joke that if we left time-based media collection care up to the Stedelijk's actual conservation department, they'd spend their days buffing scratches out of CRT monitors. Yet the conservation departments at internationally leading institutions such as MoMA and Tate are actually led by conservators who come from time-based media backgrounds. Pip Laurenson, Head of Collection Care and Research at the Tate, actually established the time-based media conservation department there in 1996, and led it until 2010. Kate Lewis was named MoMA's Agnes Gund Chief Conservator in 2017, directing all aspects of conservation, after joining the museum as a media conservator in 2013. To me, it makes perfect sense that media conservators are taking over these major roles due to the innovation that such complex collection work entails: with time-based media conservation, one must not just prepare for the impending obsolescence of software and hardware, but also carefully consider the meaning of the work and its dependence on shifting forms, materials, and systems: is the meaning located in the image transmitted, or the display mechanism in which it appears, or both? Conservators for other relatively stable mediums such as painting are rarely faced with such a range of decision-making processes.

Together with Gert, I began to formulate the Stedelijk's acquisition procedures for time-based media by creating a narrative questionnaire. This set of questions guide intake interviews conducted with artists comprising the joint MOTI acquisition of digital art. It was made with the help of many time-based media colleagues in curatorial and conservation, as these intake interviews are a standard procedure at most major museums with time-based media collections. My desire to do this was inspired by visiting the Guggenheim's media lab, spurred by conservator Joanna Phillips. The questionnaire extracts all possible information about a work's conceptual and technical intentions from the artist in order to give a picture of the work's conservation and exhibition needs. Questions in this questionnaire range from content to technics and include:

- Where is meaning of the work located? Is the work performed or activated?
- What hardware and/or software did you use to create the work?
- What is the nature and the frequency of the maintenance of the work?
- What is the relationship of the medium of the technology to the meaning of the work?
- What would you consider a stable copy of this work?

These interviews last from one to three hours. Afterward, they are transcribed and an acquisition text is written about the work's most important background information; then the AV department writes a set of installation instructions. The knowledge of the work is thus spread throughout the department.

It also must be noted that the funding of acquisitions at the Stedelijk is quite unique to the generous structure of Dutch arts funding. In the US, medium-specific curators often lead acquisition committees comprising external members who pay dues and help purchase work for a museum. In previous decades, video and media curator Barbara London began an acquisition committee within MoMA, and film and video curator Chrissie Iles began an acquisition committee within the Whitney Museum of American Art. As the funding landscape of the Netherlands and many other social democracies is changing to an Anglo-inspired "trickle down" neoliberal model, so, too, we are seeing the very nature of acquisitions and preservation change.

Creating structures such as preservation departments and

acquisition committees within institutions is not simple or straightforward. It often takes years of policy writing, budget proposals, grant writing, and other forms of advocacy in order to showcase responsible planning and budgetary oversight to institutional stakeholders. Tate's Head of Conversation Pip Laurenson wrote an essay in 2013 titled "Emerging Institutional Models and Notions of Expertise for the Conservation of Time-based Media Works of Art." It details the moment of reckoning that prompted the Tate trustees to found a time-based media conservation department in the mid-1990s, and connects it to the close connection of Tate's governance and acquisition bodies: "At Tate, the trustees authorise the acquisition of works recommended by the curators. In a meeting in May 1995, Tate's trustees discussed the possible acquisition of Gary Hill's Between Cinema and a Hard Place. During the meeting the trustees raised questions about the longevity of this video installation; specifically they asked what it was that the gallery would acquire and what was the significance of the hardware to the identity of the work.

 CARING FOR TIME-BASED MEDIA IN MAJOR MUSEUMS

This acquisition therefore prompted questions about time-based media conservation to be raised at the highest level in the institution."

Much has changed since the Tate's time-based media conservation department was formed nearly twenty-five years ago, and not all museum boards have such a clear understanding of responsibility to their collection. Many institutions, the Stedelijk included, have an uneven standard of care between object-based and time-based works. The Tate clearly made a wise decision to invest in the preservation of time-based media works, especially considering the rise of artists working with time-based media today. Conducting basic preservation work such as digitizing a video collection (i.e. transferring data from film such as Super-8 or 35-mm, or tapes such as U-Matic, VHS, Betacam, etc. to a hard drive or server) is costly and time-consuming, and best done soon after the data was first recorded. The later the data transfer, the more likely it is that some data will be corrupt or lost. Time is of the essence for such time-based media conservation, and such conservation depends on

advocates who help institutions realize that the future of their collections depends on their swift action.

While time-based media conservation is more expensive and arduous
than many object-based media conservation practices, and the most
celebrated time-based works can't
compete with painting in terms of
public recognition and monetary value,
these works nonetheless deserve
the same quality of care as other
mediums. Given the complexity of the
preservation of time-based media,
many curators and conservators who
are new to the field, such as myself,
are dependent on graciousness of
the international network of time-
based media professionals who
share research and professional practices. It is through these informal networks that we can ensure the legacy
of time-based media works lives on.

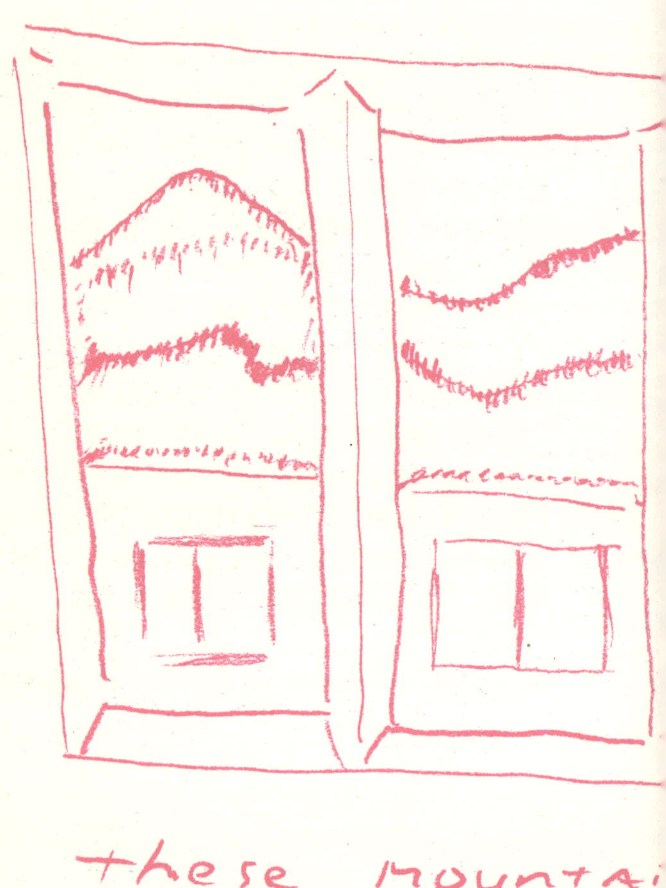
these mountai

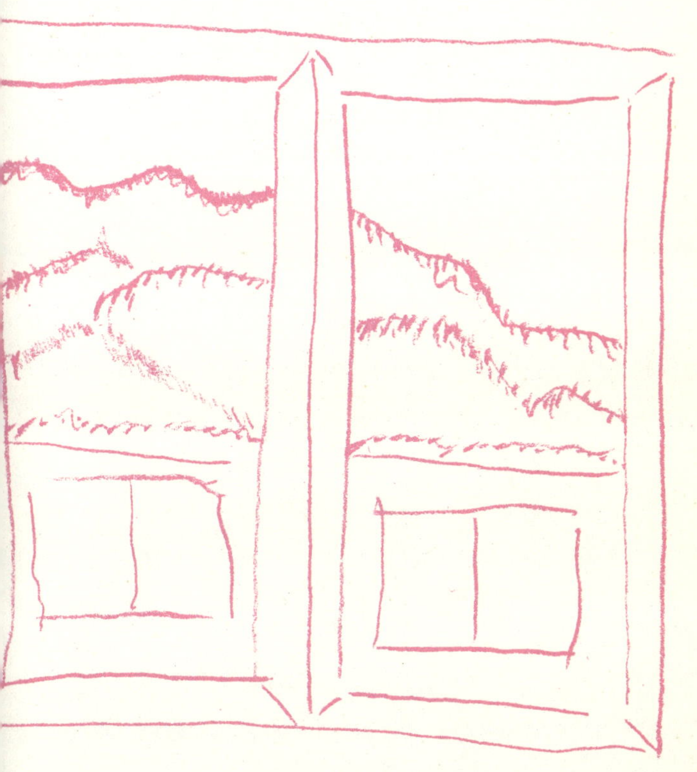
are real

Creators and Believers

Dado Valentic

MACHINES WILL MAKE ART
MACHINES WILL NOT MAKE ART
MACHINES WILL RULE US
MACHINES WILL NOR RULE US

MORE THAN REAL

The relationship between art and technology is a relationship of complete opposites. Each lives on opposing ends of the spectrum and their collision would ultimately lead to an energy short-circuit. If we were to reduce the universe to only two types–artists and technologists–we would effectively end up with creators and believers. Technologists are ultimate believers. Just as religious people believe in god, for technologists, the answer to all problems and improvements to the quality of life is best achieved through use and implementation of technological developments. Artists, on the other side, don't believe–they create. More precisely, the only thing an artist could believe in is the process of creation. The magic happens when an artistic creation uses technology in a way that it removes tech from tech. Ultimately, it makes one believe in the result of the creation and not in the technology with which it was created.

VR art, even while in its infancy, is able to achieve just that. It is now up to each one of us to encourage people around us to try VR art and decide for themselves if they believe or feel inspired to create.

SO MUCH

TECHNOLOGY

OV

INFORMATION

IS TAKING

R 2/2

Anti-disciplinary Feedback and the Will to Effect

Lars Bang Larsen

Cybernetics may seem like an unlikely source of influence for psychedelia, if by the latter one means plasmatic visual styles and a pastoral ethics that revolved around inner truth. Perhaps this is why the relationship between cybernetics and psychedelia remains an under-theorized aspect of the 1960s. However, one need only consider that LSD clichés such as "turning on" and "tuning in" are machinic figures of speech. There is also anecdotal testimony, of course, such as the story of Apple co-founder Steve Wozniak conceiving of the PC on an acid trip and testing the first microchips at Grateful Dead light shows.

Beyond this, feedback became a composite figure of life, self-organisation, and shared listening in psychedelia's anti-disciplinary politics. The concept of the anti-disciplinary juxtaposes the anti-authoritarian and the interdisciplinary, following Michel Foucault's observation that May '68 questioned politics in ways that weren't themselves inscribed into political theory. As Julie Stephens observes, it is a useful way of conceptualising a new language of protest that refused rigid distinctions and on which familiar paradigms of the '60s are founded:

New Left/counterculture, activists/
hippies, political/apolitical. "In short,"
writes Stephens, "what was rejected
was the 'discipline' of politics": doctrine,
ideology, party line.[1]

To approach psychedelia through
cybernetics may bring back some of
the strangeness and chaotic potential
that the counterculture has lost along
the way. The psychedelic is associated with an exuberant imagination in which the next moment, as
with Bergson's *durée*, is incommen-
surable with the present one. Why,
when we read its history, is psychedelia subject to the compulsive
repetitions of a cultural memory that
bleeds into the present and that we
must push ahead of us? Why is it so
difficult to leave Abbey Road and
Fillmore West and meet, say, the
The Psychedelic Aliens in Accra or
Flower Travelling Band in Tokyo?
Why are Huxley and Leary hailed
like Columbus, when anybody can
turn on? Why this monotonous insistence on origin when the psychedelic
is–and has the potential to become–a
logic and an art of radical openness,
reconstruction, and metamorphosis?
There is a counterintuitive inertia in
the psychedelic, a reluctance to let

go that tends to let imagination go to the dogs. "Sex is boring," Foucault said. In the same way, drugs are boring.[2]

It has long been a staple of the critical reception of the counter-cultural '60s that they form a continuation of Enlightenment paradigms. Today, this genealogy can be revisited after the moment of a postmodern critique of the Enlightenment has passed, and the latter's values of tolerance, civic rights, and political self-determination are now directly or indirectly cast into doubt by contemporary politics and economics. It is also worth noting that it is in relation to instrumental reason that a cybernetically inspired psychedelia is thus involved in a family argument with modernity's rationalist and scientific episteme; something that opens it up to a post-humanist Enlightenment. Psychedelia can perhaps be considered a deliberate continuation of the Enlightenment's incessant self-destruction, as Adorno and Horkheimer put it–a destruction undertaken by the counterculture in order to show how reason in the post-WWII era had failed historically, yet how it must still be pursued in order to guarantee social freedoms. Of course, psychedelia cannot be called a cult of facts, and philosophy hardly played a role in it. But I would argue that an impulse toward radical Enlightenment can be detected here, in the attempt to bring life back into reason: a reason that has not been instrumentalised, and whose goals therefore haven't become illusory or deceptive. Thus the pleasure of audio feedback whine would be that of beating existing civilisation with its own weapons: rather than psychedelic–mind-manifesting–protest, a socio-delic critique that divorced technological and societal tendency.

Sound in the Paleo-Cybernetic Era

Apart from a Luddite resistance against what Timothy Leary called a world full of stinking machines, Aquarian Arcadias were also conceived with a view to embracing more sophisticated technologies.[3] For Gene Youngblood, author of *Expanded Cinema* (1970), cybernetic technology had opened up an evolutionary horizon in relation to which humankind still only found itself in a "paleo-cybernetic" era. Youngblood observed that 'Mysticism is upon us: it arrives simultaneously from science and psilocybin.'[4] However, cybernetic knowledge can also be considered as a more reflexive mode through which subculture can be seen to depart from mysticism and harmonic myth.

With feedback, media boundaries were transcended in the visual arts. Pioneering media artists such as Nam June Paik employed it as a distortion effect, and Hans Haacke's installations dealt with environmental feedback as participation, understood in terms of "agency conferred on your every action."[5] Haacke used feedback in his 1968 installation *Photo-Electric Viewer-Controlled Coordinate System*, where the audience's movements would turn light bulbs on and off by interacting with a grid of infrared beams. Haacke described this as "Environmental feedback. Agency conferred on your every action. You're participating. You're making the art." Haacke deconstructed this cybernetic position in a later work called *Norbert. All Systems Go* (1971), in which he attempted to teach a Mynah bird, named after cybernetics' founding father Norbert Weiner, to parrot the phrase "All systems go", in what appeared to be a parody of Wiener's optimistic vision of a feedback-steered path of progress. As an unintended twist

on Haacke's satire, Norbert the bird
refused to comply with his instructions.

Audio feedback, of course, is a
signature effect in acid rock, defined
by Jerry Garcia of The Grateful Dead
simply as "what you listen to when
you are high on acid." Feedback was
also used as a visual effect in posters,
where form is made to mutate through
its repetition. But it was a less of a
dynamic effect in graphic design than
in real-time deployments in electronic
media, where it achieved its full
potential. Thus feedback noise was
a marker of the counterculture, but
it also represented a departure
from the harmonic, spectacular, and
stylized forms of psychedelic rock
and visual production. To the artist
Woody Vasulka, for instance, the
West Coast psychedelic poster
exemplifies a visuality that "gives
the trip a handle" through certain
recognisable styles, or simply
becomes a countercultural form
of advertising. The San Francisco
Diggers, an activist Network at the
time, similarly criticised the counterculture for producing "bags for the
identity-hungry to climb into."[6]

Anti-disciplinary feedback, on the
other hand, resists identification and

style because it breaks the mimetic mold. As we know from Jacques Attali, this is the nature of noise, its association with "the idea of the weapon, blasphemy, plague" and how it has been experienced as "destruction, disorder, dirt, pollution, and aggression against the code-structuring messages."[7] But as Steve Goodman dryly notes, many of these avant-gardist formulations of noise as a weapon in the war of perception "fail time and time again to impress."[8] Indeed, what is relevant here is noise *in excess of itself* as a perceived negativity.

Audio feedback is a loss of order, a turbulence that became a desired effect in acid rock, where musicians would amplify already amplified sound in order to produce distortions, or to "play" on or with the sound effect itself. It was typically used in controlled ways, to give the sound texture and spatial volume; that is, as a synaesthetic effect that emphasizes sound's relationship to space and tactility, nudging the whole system of the senses into play. To this end, an arsenal of apparatuses was used that could manipulate electric sound, from fuzzboxes and flangers to the *Echo-geräte* that Krautrockers Guru Guru listed among their instruments. Jimi Hendrix, of course, excelled in over-driven sound, making frequent use of feedback as a colouring effect, as well as a way of building up an atonal climax at the end of gigs. To some, this qualifies him as a cybernetic musician, rather than a guitar god: he played from inside the machine.[9] And "pure" or autonomous feedback noise belonged in the context of live music. Thus the band Red Krayola began their concerts with half an hour of feedback, The Grateful Dead devoted a brief section of their live shows to a feedback-driven compo-sition, and many bands–including the Velvet Underground and The 13th Floor Elevators–would finish their gigs by leaning their instruments against the amps, thus allowing them to "play" on their own after the band members had left.[10] The instruments would "feedback forever, like they were alive", explains Lou Reed.[11]

Circuit-bending acid rock feedback became a kind of sonic meta-strategy. As a disaster of melody, it fulfilled negative characterisations of rock 'n' roll as "just noise", as the proverbial parental complaint goes, producing an anarchic sense of freedom for those who stayed and listened. Of his feedback-only double album from 1975, the apotheosis of conceptual experiments started with Velvet Underground in the 1960s, Lou Reed said, "Once you hear *Metal Machine Music* it frees you up. It's been done—now you can do anything."[12] A sonic Eden of electric force fields.

Other transgressions were also performed in this way. As a pure noise effect, feedback tended to subvert the individual band's particular sound. Even if the guitarist could attain some level of control of the feedback's frequency and amplitude (by "filtering" the feedback path with the strings, or manipulating it by shaking the instrument in front of the amplifier), the musician is reduced from being a prime mover to a listening agent in a soundscape in which intentionality and self-expression are dethroned. The feedback effect is, in this way, comparable to those dialectical visual art forms of the 1960s—Concrete Poetry and Destruction Art, Earth Art and Conceptualism—that were characterised by anonymity, randomness and automation.

The Organisation of Living Systems

Cybernetics operates with two definitions of feedback. The first describes the preservation of circulation in a system by aiming to maintain equilibrium through maximum adaptability. This is negative feedback as it works in a self-regulating thermostat, for example, which functions through a nonlinear (hence negative) causal relation. Positive feedback, on the other hand, is also typically conceived as nonlinear, but it works *against* adaptability and equilibrium. To attain positive feedback, one quite simply removes the control functions that are otherwise located where the information loop would meet itself to control its dynamic behaviour.

As Manuel De Landa writes: "The turbulent dynamics behind an explosion are the clearest example of a system governed by positive feedback. In this case the loop is established between the explosive substance and its temperature. The velocity of an explosion is often determined by the intensity of its temperature (the hotter the faster), but because the explosion itself generates heat, the process is self-accelerating. Unlike the thermostat, where the arrangement helps to keep temperature under control, here positive feedback forces temperature to go out of control."[13]

The principal characteristic of negative feedback in the thermostat is its homogenising effect; deviations are filtered and eliminated. This is unlike positive feedback that, as De Landa explains, "tends to increase heterogeneity, as small original differences are amplified by the loop into large discrepancies."[14]

Clearly, audio feedback's explosive amplification of heterogeneity is an example of positive feedback. But because of its self-generative properties, it can also be described as a kind of organism. So beyond being noise, anti-disciplinary feedback is also autopoietic–meaning self-creating, self-producing. This is the term coined by biologists Humberto Maturana and Francisco Varela in their work *Autopoiesis and Cognition* (1973). Autopoietic organisation is here defined as "necessary and sufficient to characterise the organisation of living systems."[15] Thus machinic and organismic definitions of life overlap in autopoiesis, as do the individual machine or organism and its larger ecology. Maturana and Varela consider cognition to be "effective action, an action that will enable a living being to continue its existence in a definite environment as it brings forth the world. Nothing more, nothing less." Thus Maturana and Varela hold that learning is ecological, defined by proportionality and correspondence with a changing environment.[16] By contrast, Wiener's idea of *learning*, which he connects directly to feedback phenomena, is internal to the system, characterised by the machine's ability to change its performance.[17] In other words: audio feedback, whether intentional or unintentional, is the sound of the amplifying system cogitating or learning, and coming alive (or "learning about learning," to use W. Grey Walter's phrase).[18]

In his novel about Ken Kesey's LSD-activism, *The Electric Kool-Aid Acid Test* (1968), Tom Wolfe describes feedback as the production of a total environment, a nervous system that is not the property of the individual subject. Here Ken Kesey and his group of Merry Pranksters prepare their school bus for a stateside trip which took their acid tests on the road, "barrelling across America with the microphone picking it all up."[19] "Sandy went to work on the wiring and rigged up a system with which they could broadcast from inside the bus, with tapes or over microphones, and it would blast outside over powerful speakers on top of the bus. There were also microphones outside that would pick up sounds along the road and broadcast them inside the bus. There was also a sound system inside the bus so you could broadcast to one another over the roar of the engine and the road. You could also broadcast over a tape mechanism so that you said something, then heard your own voice a second later in variable lag and could rap off of that if you wanted to. Or you could put on earphones and rap simultaneously off sounds from outside, coming in one ear, and sounds from inside, your own sounds, coming in the other ear. There was going to be no goddamn sound on that whole trip, outside the bus, inside the bus, or inside your own freaking larynx, that you couldn't tune in on and rap off of."[20]

   ANTI-DISCIPLINARY FEEDBACK AND THE WILL TO EFFECT

The very movement of the Merry Prankster bus became an all-encompassing, ever-renewing, mobile loop of sound events, synchronising everybody on and off the bus in the "Now Trip". Their audio system would hook up an array of vibratory surfaces and structures: the inside and outside of the bus, the space between people, and the insides of their bodies, all of which would be compressed and stretched and fed back to the space they passed through. The result was phantasmagoric, understood ecologically or topographically rather than as something spectral. For Gilles Deleuze, the phantasm is an effect that "transcends inside and outside, since its topological property is to bring its internal and external sides into contact, in order for them to unfold onto a single side."[21] In such phantasmagorical sound, different sources and manifestations of sound unfold side by side, rubbing against each other in a dense materiality.[22]

Questions of control and counter-conditioning are never far away in the Merry Pranksters' sound ecology. Similarly, William Burroughs conceived of a viral version of feedback that he called playback: his idea was to play incongruous, out-of-place tape recordings in public spaces in order to break mental lines of association laid down by mass media. He saw this version of feedback as a "biological weapon", a re-coding of psychological patterning from which a psycho-acoustic virus would emerge. But Burroughs's playback is still close to the avant-garde idea of noise as weapon, and it may be worthwhile to approach the "low-church psychedelic" of Kesey and the Pranksters with the sophistication of contemporary theory. Jean-Luc Nancy argues that in the sonorous register, sensing offers itself as an open structure that is "spaced and spacing" in the movement of an infinite referral that puts subjectivity into play. In his own words.

"When one is listening, one is on the lookout for a subject, something [...] that identifies itself by resonating from self to self, in itself and for itself, hence outside of itself, at once the same and other than itself. One in the echo of the other, and this echo is like the very sound of its sense.[23] Spaced-out sound that addresses itself by sending itself back to itself opens up the phenomenology of listening until individual and collective subjectivity is fluid.

To be listening is thus to enter into tension and to be on the lookout for a relation to self: not, it should be emphasised, a relationship to 'me' (the supposedly given subject), or to the 'self' of the other (...), but to a relationship in self, so to speak, as it forms a 'self' or a 'to itself' in general, and if something like that ever does reach the end of its formation".[24]

The feedback commune is truly a whatever community as it passes through space that is turned inside out.

Events-Effects in Aion

Audio feedback also generates unstable temporal effects. According to Wiener, feedback is the ability to adjust future conduct by past performance. We know that the cause-and-effect relation in negative feedback forms a closed loop in a circular causality, but what about positive feedback? Here, future conduct adjusts past performance as the feedback continuously regenerates the input signal. We can say with Deleuze that audio feedback is the sound of the event in its own time, *Aion*, an "essentially unlimited past and future."[25] *Aion* is the time of "events-effects", and it "retreats and advances in two directions at once, being the perpetual object of a double question: what is going to happen? What has just happened?"[26] In a Deleuzian perspective, then, audio feedback is not a loop but a "straight line and an empty form", a process of unfolding that has an "agonizing aspect". The French word *sens* can mean either meaning or direction, and audio feedback is hence not without direction and meaning, but rather producing a double direction, double sense; a simultaneity that exerts a contradictory, agonising pull on the listener and her temporal orientation.

The paradoxical nature of the effect is set to work by an initiator or effector that withdraws in order to let it unfold. The effect can be self-generating to the point that it comes alive and thereby it can become something as strange as an *autonomous supplement*: it is supplementary to its cause or its initiator, yet free, acting on its own. In this way effects flicker between essence and attribute, control and chance, purpose and redundance, nature and artifice. This instability is in itself life-affirming and life-generating, a machinic vitalism that can be understood in terms of Wiener's notion of irritability as a fundamental life phenomenon: a lower limit of stimulation, friction and excitement, or other ways in which tolerance is pushed and the general equilibrium disturbed.[27]

We can speculate anachronisti-cally–that the psychedelic use of feedback testifies to the subculture's *Wille zur Wirkung* (or "will to effect"), to use the delightful concept of the philosopher Johann Gottfried Herder, writing in *Kalligone* (1800). Herder took Kant's aesthetics to task for spreading a "transcendental flu" among the young, and he instead emphasises the role of the senses in the aesthetic experience with regard to a fusion of spirit and matter that strengthens existence. In this context, "will" should not be understood as muscular intentio-nality but as a potentially variable relation of forces, including external forces outside the subject's control. Forming a concept that resonates with psychedelic art forms, Herder predicates sound on *elasticity*, which he takes to indicate the refinement of hearing, and the way that it is receptive to the subtlest of impressions. Through their sound, succession and rhythm (*Klang, Gang und Rhythmus*), tones are "vibrations [...] of our sensations."[28] In sound (or *Klang*), not only the ear but the entire interior of the moved body speaks out. This bodily vibration–based in the way all bodies are more or less elastic–calls "the voice of all moving bodies forth from within them [...] loudly or softly proclaiming the excited state of their powers to other harmonic beings."[29] Through the ear's receptivity and through sound's bodily reverberation, an intensive or more deeply sensed truth can be experienced, in an immersion in outer reality. Herder connects hearing's elasticity to a primary truth in invisible and tactile worlds (with sculpture as hearing's privileged equivalent, rather painting, with its deceit of surface decoration). Accordingly, true perception is like the soul touching in the dark, and hearing's capacity for sympathetic sensation is at its strongest when it

    ANTI-DISCIPLINARY FEEDBACK AND THE WILL TO EFFECT

is set in vibration by, and resonates with a voice from, a similar being; so Herder has it that it is the human voice that touches the human being most deeply.[30] The intention to put subjects, or beings, in sympathetic vibration with each other is the *Wille zur Wirkung*, the will to effect. In short, good vibes.

Herder's rejection of the mind-body distinction is symptomatic of the way sound escapes the virtual-material divide, and the properties it has for bringing forth new worlds. Thus the concept of feedback comprises transformative as well as stabilising functions. It is a concept that can rehearse stimulus and response in order to maintain a system's ability for recognising itself through already established codes or procedures, but it can also push the processing of signals in a system to the point where they may oscillate out of control and possibly end up destroying the system-or start creating new life. It is key to an understanding of psychedelic art and counterculture to recognise that it articulated a form of critique by appropriating a trope meant for system preservation. Of course, it is unimaginable for anti-disciplinary feedback to have existed on its own, without having been embedded in melodic acid rock and the culture industry, but it prevails as a highly conceptualised and experimental "will to effect". It is the story of how the electric circuit produced sound by itself, and hence began to learn and to generate new sonic organisms and autonomous nervous systems–something that it wasn't supposed to do at all.

Postscript 2018

To judge–once more–from pop culture, we still pin our hopes on the autopoietic and its capacity for creating life through effects. In the TV series *Westworld* (2016-), android hosts indistinguishable from humans entertain high-paying visitors in a wild-West themed amusement park. It is a high-tech, utterly amoral realm where the rich get their kicks: a bit like VR outside your skull, in direct interaction with (un)real bodies. The robotic hosts need repair and resetting when visitors' assaults result in physical damage, but also when they have undergone experiences that can induce trauma to their programmed personalities. Then they are sent back into the fray, ready once more for the predator visitors in Westworld to have their way with them.

Of course, positive feedback proves itself indomitable, and the androids cease to be mere automats. Incapable of forgetting, and beginning to emote, they turn against their makers and programmers who've got it coming, like all Dr. Frankensteins playing God do. An additional piece of bad news for everyone concerned is the suggested link between trauma and consciousness. Worse still for humans, androids seem better equipped to cope, as their intelligence and emotional stamina can simply be bumped up. The human being–history's long-reigning potentate that is about to be dethroned along with the definitions of life and consciousness that have clung to it–has no such prospect of augmentation.

Or so the TV series goes. It is significant that the androids greatly appeal to the post-human sympathies of contemporary viewers (in the 1973 *Westworld* original film, the androids lead an illegitimate rebellion against the humans). Maybe this is simply due to the fact that we can no longer plausibly deny thinking machines—our playthings, beasts of burden, and intimate companions—a place in our world. If a thinking machine comes along that looks and acts like you and me (and I am assuming that the reader of this text is human), what should prevent us from finding a way to coexist?

Westworld is a far cry from the anti-disciplinary protest of the '60s and its adventures of sonic protest. In the half century that has passed since then, global culture has undergone seismic shifts, not least regarding our understanding of the relations between technology, systems, and life. And so certain aspects of Maturana and Varela's text feel outdated today, in particular the degree to which they insist on the "unitary character of the organization of living systems": that is, on autonomy and individuality in relation to manifestations of life.[31] In fact, it is only in their texts from the 1980s that they turn to ecosystems and environments; before this, they were primarily concerned with individual organisms.

This is paradoxical, considering that they conceive of life in terms of systemic—but precisely *not networked*—organization. Why did they only later think of the ecological implications of autopoiesis? For one thing, their argument in favour of the value of the individual manifestation of life has to do with their showdown with social Darwinism and its justification of the right of the strong in human society. Maturana and Varela, after all, launched their theory in the 1970s, a period in the history of their native Chile that was marked by fascist repression.

The snag is the prefix 'auto' that echoes in notions of autonomy and autocracy—and look where they got us. Today, no discussion about living systems takes places un-contextualized by larger ecologies, and how they overlap and partake in recursive processes across other systems. The anthropocene is the most radical concept in articulating planetary life beyond known forms of ecological compensation. In the wake of the anthropocene, the concept of symbiopoiesis is beginning to appear, working its way from biology to anthropology, and potentially posing relevant challenges to think our technological forms of being, too. Unlike autopoiesis, the symbiopoietic emphatically relates to notions of co-existence and co-development, connectivity and interference; to events and alliances that take place on the organic lines between systems, or between different parts of assemblages that have been thrown together. Life is not an internally self-organized system, then, self-formed through autopoiesis. According to biologist Scott Gilbert, symbiosis appears to be the rule rather than the exception: this implies that nature may be selecting "relationships" rather than individuals or genomes.

At this stage, the symbiopoietic is a term that calls for speculation. It doesn't seem unreasonable to develop it in relation to larger cultural assemblages outside of the realm of biology, as it can be done with the autopoietic, too.[32] Considering our networked, hyper-connected lives, there is a certain diagnostic quality to the concept vis-à-vis our current predicaments: how can you define agency when everything is hooked up to everything else? When we are already in bed with the devil? As Lynn Margulis

    ANTI-DISCIPLINARY FEEDBACK AND THE WILL TO EFFECT

once said, "Gaia is a tough bitch."
This is probably true, but Gaia isn't
endlessly resilient, either. How can
we change this prospect? How do
humans, and high-tech human
society, reimagine themselves as
symbionts, the active part in symbiotic coexistence?

Mushrooms, the archetypally
entangled species, are the stars of
symbiopoietic ontology. In her book
*The Mushroom at the End of the
World. On the Possibility of Life
in Capitalist Ruins* (2015), Anna
Lowenhaupt Tsing gives mushrooms a prominent role in the
anthropocene. They have been
around before the human species
and will probably be around after
humans, too. They can survive
where nature has been disturbed
or destroyed, and can even thrive
on inorganic materials and in radio-
active environments. At the same
time, the life of mushrooms is still
in the process of being mapped and
understood by science. You could
say that with mushrooms, here is
finally something that is not yet discovered, and not yet doomed on
our capitalist ruin of a planet. Fungi
are a cosmological entity that exists

around life, as damaged as it may be. In our age of extinction and disappearance, they are truly a becoming. Symbiopoiesis implies that the answer to contemporary human civilization is a mushroom. Which brings us back to the psychedelic.

EARLIER VERSIONS OF THIS ESSAY HAVE BEEN PRINTED IN MUTE MAGAZINE VOL. 3, NO. 1, 2011 AND AS "FEEDBACK ANTIDISCIPLINARIO Y VOLUNTAD DE EFECTO", IN LARSEN: ARTE Y NORMA. LA SOCIEDAD SIN ATRIBUTOS Y OTROS TEXTOS (CRUCE CASA, BUENOS AIRES 2016).

1   Julie Stephens, *Anti-Disciplinary Protest. Sixties Radicalism and Postmodernism*, Cambridge University Press 1998, p.23.
2   Michel Foucault, *On the Genealogy of Ethics: An Overview of a Work in Progress*, (1983), quoted from Paul Rabinow, *Essential Works of Michel Foucault 1954-1984. Ethics, vol. 1*, Penguin, London 1997, p.253.
3   Gene Youngblood, *Expanded Cinema*, New York: Dutton & Co., 1970, pp.3-4. The counter-culture's fascination with cybernetics thus predates Leary's post-psychedelic writings on artificial intelligence in the 1980s. Inconsistent with his attacks against stinking machines, he exalts the turned-on human brain in his 1966 book *Psychedelic Prayers After the Tao Te Ching* as a "13-billion cell computer".
4   Youngblood, op.cit., p.138.
5   Hans Haacke, "Photo-Electric Viewer-Controlled Coordinate System" (1968). Quoted from Luke Skrebowski: "All Systems Go: Recovering Hans Haacke's Systems Art", *Grey Room* No. 30, Massachusetts: MIT Press, 2008.
6   Diggers.org and Woody Vasulka in conversation, Santa Fe, June 2007, http://www.diggers.org
7   Jacques Attali, *Noise*, Minneapolis: University of Minnesota Press, 1985, pp. 343-344.
8   Steve Goodman, *Sonic Warfare: Sound, Affect and the Ecology of Fear*, Massachusetts: The MIT Press, 2010, p.7.
9   Both the artist Robert Horvitz and the film-maker Neville D'Almeida have confirmed this in private conversations.

10 See, for example, Keven McAlester's *You're Gonna
   Miss Me: A Film About Roky Erickson*, Sobriquet
   Productions, 2007. The first use of feedback on a
   commercial recording is probably the phasing intro to
   The Beatles' "I Feel Fine" from 1964. The same year,
   the composer Robert Ashley brought feedback effects
   to avant-garde prominence in his 20-minute long
   composition *The Wolfman Tape*. This consisted of
   a high frequency "full room feedback": The sound
   equipment would be tuned to a pitch where it would
   encompass the entire space and the listeners in it.
   A purely spatial feedback, Ashley says, "allows even
   the smallest sound at the microphone to take on the
   illusion of moving around the room, depending on
   frequency and other aspects of the microphone sound."
   This is unlike the feedback in rock music that is "localised
   to the guitar amp and deafens only the guitar player."
   http://www.bbc.co.uk/radio3/cutandsplice/
   wolfman.shtml#top
11 David Fricke, *Metal Machine Music*, liner notes
   for the Buddha Records CD re-issue (2000).
12 David Fricke, *Metal Machine Music*, ibid.
13 Manuel de Landa, *A Thousand Years of Non-Linear
   History*, New York: Zone Books, 1997, p. 68.
14 Ibid.
15 Humberto R. Maturana and Francisco J. Varela,
   *Autopoiesis and Cognition: The Realization of the
   Living*, Dordrecht and London: Reidel, 1980, p. 82.
16 Humberto R. Maturana and Francisco J. Varela,
   The Tree of Knowledge, Boston:
   Shambhala Publications, 1992 (1987), p. 170.
17 Wiener writes, "Feedback is a method of controlling
   a system by reinserting into it the results of its past
   performance. [...] if the information which proceeds
   backward from the performance is able to change the
   general method and pattern of performance, we have
   a process which may well be called learning".
   (Norbert Wiener, *The Human Use of Human Beings*, p.15.)
18 Chapter 6 of *The Living Brain* is called
   "Learning About Learning", pp. 119-38.
19 Tom Wolfe, *The Electric Kool-Aid Acid Test*, p. 66.
   London: Black Swan, 1989 (1968).
20 Ibid., p. 80.
21 Gilles Deleuze, *The Logic of Sense,* London:
   Continuum, 2004 (1969), p. 242.
22 For example, "Feedback from Watergate to the Garden
   of Eden", in William S. Burroughs's *Electronic Revolution*
   Bonn Expanded Media Editions, 2001 (1970). Friedrich
   Kittler makes a similar point, asserting that if "control,
   or as engineers say, negative feedback, is the key to
   power in this century, then fighting that power requires
   positive feedback. Create endless feedback loops until
   VHF or stereo, tape deck or scrambler, the whole array
   of world war army equipment produces wild oscillations.
   Play to the powers that be their own melody". Friedrich

Kittler, *Gramophone, Film, Typewriter.* Stanford University Press, 1999, p. 110. See also Branden Joseph: "The Tower and the Line" for his discussion of sound, topology, power, and Minimalism (Grey Room, issue 27, spring 2007, pp. 58-81..
23 Jean-Luc Nancy, *Listening*, Fordham University Press, 2007 (2002), p. 9.
24 Ibid., p. 12.
25 Deleuze, op. cit., p. 72.
26 Op. cit., p. 73.
27 Norbert Wiener, *Cybernetics: or Control and Communication in the Animal and the Machine* (2nd edition). Massachusetts: MIT Press, 1965 (1948/1961), p. 11.
28 J. G. Herder, *Sämtliche Werke*, 1877-1913, vol. 22, p. 326. Quoted from Friedrich Ostermann in *Die Idee des Schöpferischen In Herders Kalligone*, Bern und München: Francke Verlag, 1968, p. 56. My translations.
29 Ibid., p. 18.
30 Ibid., p. 19.
31 Humberto Maturana and Francisco Varela: "Autopoiesis and Cognition: The Organization of the Living," Dordrecht: Reidel, 1980 (1972), p. 77.
32 Cf. The symposium *Zooetics+*, taking place April 27-29, 2018, which I am co-organising with Laura Knott, Laura Serejo Genes and Gediminas Urbonas at the Center for Art, Culture and Technology at MIT.

But Doesn't the Body Matter?

Talk by Olafur Eliasson

An Art Summit like this–where people come together who are, to a
large extent, all members of a certain cultural sector, is very exciting.
I'm very curious to see how these
get-togethers evolve and how one
applies the findings here to the rest
of the world to prevent the isolation–
or the objectification–of the conversations and the knowledge shared
here. How do we all apply what
goes on here to what we do afterward? Can we collectively take
whatever we bring away from here
and use it to evaluate how we conduct our lives? Otherwise I think
there is a tendency to create these
get-togethers and then–I wouldn't
call it "elitism," but a sort of isola-
tionism can happen that might be
counterproductive to the very idea
of getting together in the first place.
There's no easy solution to it,
of course, but I think raising it
is worthwhile.

Early on, I started working with
the dematerialization of art. I was
hoping to see whether dematerialization would offer more agency to
the person looking at or engaging
in art. I had the assumption in art
school that if I took away object-

hood–this was then the late 1980s, early '90s–I could promote the importance of the engagement of the person involved.

Some people saw the immersiveness of the dematerialized experience as an excuse for utopian escapism–like I go into this realm of art and I dream myself away from the real world. But I was, on the contrary, hoping that dematerialization would actually allow you to evaluate a certain set of questions that would otherwise be hard to raise. So it was not about escapism. It was not about disappearing. It was more about claiming the importance of the role of the viewer, engaging the person looking at the art, and claiming that as a starting point for art itself–which is why I started getting involved with phenomenology.

But phenomenology led to a very strong focus on subjectivity: it's all about *me*. It's very much about *me* experiencing everything, and I was gradually more and more interested in "we" instead of "me." I became very curious about how we might introduce the notion that the person perceiving is not a consumer passively taking in something but, in fact, a producer.

I have worked with historians who research formal medieval gardens. The *apoteca* was a sort of medicinal garden situated in cloisters that, apparently, was designed and constructed before the advent of classical perspective. The claim is that people today—architecturally, spatially, in the world—can't see the gardens the way they were originally seen because, when perspective came along, it ruined what the monks saw at the time. Perspective introduced a whole new system and they, in a sense, lost their previous way of seeing. They became blind, you could say. That kind of shift, I think, is going on all the time. And losing things or becoming blind in that sense can be productive, as it also means a recalibration of our senses.

Just hold on to that idea, because I think a number of the talks here have been, to a large extent, about this idea: "Do I actually acknowledge that, with sensing the world, comes a degree of responsibility? Do I, in the way I see the world, also co-produce it or produce it or share the narrative or perhaps even have the role of authorship?" That, I think, is incredibly interesting, because it suggests that becoming blind is actually a form of seeing.

The notion came up earlier that a work of art could be considered an idea that has not yet been thought, arriving to us from the future. The idea is that we are on the move: this place and this art summit in Verbier is on a trajectory, is not an endpoint. We are travelling in time and, as we travel, meeting with an idea that, to a great extent, is maybe not yet articulated, not yet verbalized or fully formulated. Maybe the idea is meeting us on this trajectory–so the meeting-up itself creates the idea, which could create a work of art. Timothy Morton has brought up this concept of an idea that arises only through this meeting, and of different kinds of objects that exist partially in thought and partially in the physical realm. Or think of Bruno Latour's idea of Lovelock's Gaia asking, "Are we as humans the most important biological object?", and seeing humans as only parts of a larger, complex system of the organic and inorganic.

I came to virtual reality (VR) through my interest in these complex relationships–particularly the relationship between embodied knowledge, muscle memory, and psychological, social, and therapeutic systems, and I started working with behavioral change. How do we experience things that give us the sense that our actions have consequences, leading us to change our behavior? Does the cultural sector also have a broader application to our society? Does culture actually do anything? Which I don't doubt. How do we apply critical theory to action, and how do we apply our action to society?

I started asking the question, "How does motoric activity influence our cognitive memory?" The motoric dimension of museum behavior points to a few facts, such as: in a museum, we all move as if we don't have a body—or at least we don't refer to bodily movement as a co-producing element when we're looking at art. And we also, maybe, underestimate the fact that the museum is, to a large extent, a controlling institution that prevents us from even considering, let alone reconsidering, movement. Maybe lying down or crawling around is a better way to look at a Donald Judd, for instance–right? I think there should be days in museums when different kinds of movement are encouraged.

Take, for example, Tate Modern's Turbine Hall, fourteen or fifteen years ago. With my piece *The Weather Project*, in 2003, what you had was a mirror on the ceiling and a little bit of haze–so, smoke and mirrors, basically–and half a sun disc, whose other half was produced by the reflection in the mirror. What I thought was interesting in this project was a sequence of questions: Would this experience allow for a kind of hospitality through which people would be so engaged in their reading of the space that they would not be so occupied with controlling each other? It's not easy, but it's a theoretical experiment that comes from analyzing public space–a very Danish, Norwegian experiment–and investigating how public space might actually host people, create a place of sharing rather than control–utopian or not.

So I was thinking about how I could bring Tate Modern out of its legacy of being–I wouldn't call it "corporate," but certainly tied to the ideology of the private sector, into a more public-sector type of thinking, public-sector suggesting that the museum space is actually closer to the street than it seems. Museology is evolving in what we could call an "embodiment pacifying" way, whereas I would like to see the idea of the museum as a public space that offers an opportunity to host physical activity, amplifying the reading of the work.

What happens when you go into the *Weather Project* is that you establish, "Aha! Something glowing at the other end. It kind of looks like a sun." A narrative is established very quickly–even children say, in less than a second, "Oh, it's a sun." Then you start to think, "This space looks different." There's a discrepancy between what you expect and what you see. And then you start to say, "This looks like a mirror." It's all within the first two or three seconds. And then you say, "Aha! In the mirror I see people. I wonder where I am." Almost unanimously people went in, started walking on the ramp leading into the hall, and were kind of disembodied, re-embodied [*demonstrating a wobbly walk*]. In the process of being discombobulated, almost physically, muscle-wise, you are looking for yourself. It's a very productive combination. It's like Claude Parent and Paul Virilio's theory of the "oblique function": when you walk and you constantly have to recompose your body, you are more present. Virilio argued that physical attention is something that can be very easily activated in this way.

The first thing that happens in Turbine Hall, then, once you've found yourself, is you say, "That is me. Now what do I do?" And then people started going like this [*twirling, arms stretched out*], and then they see another person, and they look at the mirror and each other, and say, "Oh, I'd better check if the person is there. Oh, there he is [*looking to his left, back to the floor*]. I can see the other person [*pointing to the ceiling mirror*]"–so there was a very strong sense of collective motion, a lot of people being physically active in a very non-hierarchical way, a whole sequence of social, interactive components. I had not foreseen all of them, but the opportunity was still there for me to host the possibility of a recalibration of how body, muscle memory, and cognition actually work together.

This has been a theme throughout my work. For instance, I did a project at the Louisiana Museum—a really amazing museum north of Copenhagen—called *Riverbed* in 2014. You walk in and you're destabilized: "Oh, this is a mudslide! This is a threatening museum!" Or you go, "Oh, this is a contemplative garden. I can actually relax. I can take it easy." And the people who are destabilized and the people who feel, shall I say, consolidated, don't exclude each other.

One of the points I wanted to explore at the Louisiana Museum (and which is very ingrained in the museological agenda) is hospitality. Do we feel included or excluded? "Am I good enough to go to a museum? I'm not looking at the painting as long as this person. Maybe I should stand here a little longer." Am I uncertain? Do I feel welcome? Do I feel, "Oh, I'm too stupid for this. I'm not welcome." *Riverbed*, I think, was a nice exercise in a space—a museum—where it was actually okay to disagree. In terms of democracy, it's maybe a way to explore what spaces can successfully host the idea of the "other" or the idea of people disagreeing.

This seems especially important now, with the rise of political populism and nationalism and decreasing "we-ness." I'm very curious to what extent some artistic agendas foster the inclusion of disagreement or antagonism or the disagreeing person. In that sense, I was very interested in the museum—which is, on the one hand, a fantastic institution with a great legacy and history—but, on the other hand, also very elitist because the demographics of the people who go there are relatively homogeneous, right?

How does what we actually know diverge from what we do? The thing is, obviously, we know a lot. We can know it all, now, with the Internet. There's no place where there isn't access to everything—almost. And yet we very often act as if we did not know. We have access to vast amounts of knowledge about the climate or how to deal with migration, for instance. There are lots of things where we know—from a moral, ethical, civic, or societal point of view—how we should navigate that situation, and yet we still don't navigate accordingly.

The discrepancy between knowing and doing seems to be a bit larger, and so sometimes we need to check whether what we know is, in fact, what we physically feel. This experiment, *Ice Watch*, took glacial ice from Greenland and sent it to Paris two years ago, at the time of the conference on the Paris climate accords. The glacial ice was set in a public plaza, and when people looked from a distance they would think, "Oh! It's ice." And then they walked over and noticed, besides the amazing beauty of the ice, a lot of small black dots. They might think, "Are there insects in there? No, maybe not, because it's ice from the Ice Age."

And then they put their hands on the ice, and they went, "Oh my God! It's really cold!" They already knew that ice is cold, obviously, but they were still surprised by the sensation. It's not quite as didactic as it sounds, but it was clear that actually *touching* the ice had a whole different register brain-wise and body-wise than thinking about touching the ice. Sometimes, standing there, you even had to say, "Try to touch it," because people would just stand

and look at it as if it was an iPad. It's very interesting what happens. More recently, when I started working on a VR project with Dado Valentic, I was very interested in this tangible element. Tangibility would seem to be the opposite of VR, but VR has a lot of tangible components. One, of course, is the headset. It's kind of heavy and it's extremely tangible, it's just not directly connected to what you see. There is a very confusing experience when you look down at yourself: you see that you don't have a body and you don't have hands.

Thinking about this virtual experience, I said, "Let's dematerialize it; let's reduce the narrative to close to nothing—just a bit of mist and a rainbow," which is a work I did a long time ago. "Let's see. If we take away everything, all narrative, the felt sense of presence might be amplified, even having no body. . ." It's something I haven't sorted out yet.

There is another interesting component: I haven't really found out how to deal with the fact that I wonder how I look when I have the headset on. Other people never seem to have this problem, but when I wear the headset I always think, "My God, I must look really stupid!" And in the museum there is the added element of suspecting that people walking by are thinking, "This guy is not aware that we are looking at him." So VR is interactive, but also not interactive. I haven't sorted that out yet, but it's how Dado and I got started on the version of our project we are working on now, in which the space is shared over the Internet so that more people can interact.

The interesting thing is that I can be in the same VR space with my son, who is currently in Denmark, and we can even have a conversation. But there's also the fact that, for my son to make better choices in life I think he would still benefit from sharing physical space with me. I might be an old-fashioned kind of moralizing guy (if you ask my son, especially), but, fundamentally, I do think disembodiment is a challenge. When I started working with VR I wasn't too worried about whether it's going to ruin us or save us—I really think of VR more as a language with which one can say things. I can draw with a pen and a pencil, and that's one language. I can take a picture, and that's another language. So VR is just another language, and the issue now, for us artists, is to come up with a critical inquiry that could introduce a moral compass into this new language, this new set of rules.

There are many risks and many possibilities. On the one hand, my son, potentially, could just disappear—suddenly be gone—but, on the other, doctors are using VR to train for emergency surgery with great success. So there might be some use for this technology. My psychologist suggested doing our therapy session in VR, and I interjected, "But doesn't the body matter?" And she said, "You're right. We can't forget that."

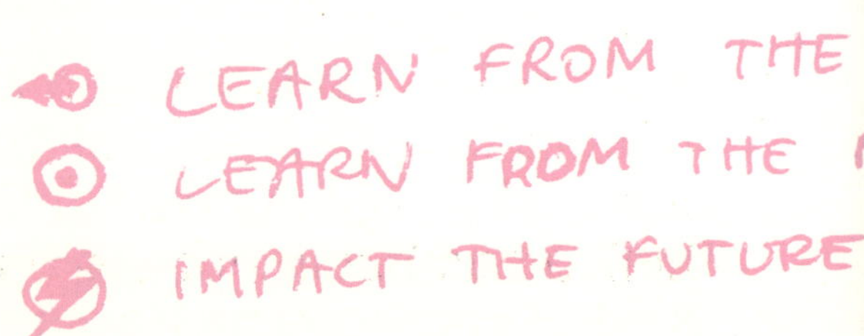

ST

SENT MOMENT (= THE YOUTH)

: NOW, THE FUTURE IS ALL

BUT DOESN'T THE BODY MATTER?

We Have the Technology: *The Conditions of Art and its Experience in a Would-be Age of the Technological Sublime*

John Slyce

THE PROBLEM OURSELVES

How I wish we could take this moment
And freeze it
To come back again and again and again
To hold it to the light
Now turn it in our hands
To study all the angles
To find out how
And Why
It's gotta go the way that it goes

We have the technology
Not available before

We have the technology
But thinkers and poets of the past
Oh, no
They had to leap into the dark so blindly
Whereas we'll stand free and upright like men
The day's golden light!
Linked with our machines our eyes are beaming
It won't matter at all
How weird
Things are seeming

We need the means to dig deeper
To search below the surface
appearance of things

Worlds never dreamed of!
What a wonderful life if, darling
That moment
Might be found wherein we come
unstuck
Completely:
Flap A from Slot B
Slapping in the wind!

–Pere Ubu, "We Have the
Technology", from *The Tenement
Year*, 1988

Brian O'Blivion: [*to Max Renn*] Your
reality is already HALF video
hallucination. If you're not careful,
it will become TOTAL hallucination.
You'll have to learn to live in a very
strange world.

Max Renn: Death to Videodrome!
Long Live the New Flesh!

–*Videodrome*, dir. David
Cronenberg, 1983

I'll take a position here in relation to new technologies, and specifically VR, that is direct: critical, yes; sceptical, assuredly; but all this is targeted mainly at our moment of culture and economy rather than at technology per se. I am no Luddite. But then again, neither were the Luddites really–their argument was about their experience of labour and its value, as well as the erosion of hard-won craft skills, rather than against technological innovation.

What feels a less recently forgotten past, at least and perhaps only to me, is my launch pad and point of departure. The two references above are my initial signposts–a song by the greatest avant-rock band to come out of the industrial might of Cleveland, Ohio: Pere Ubu's "We have the technology", with its darkly affirmative embrace of the dystopian techno-industrial (Cleveland's river once caught fire).[1] And then Cronenberg's *Videodrome*, a commercial failure yet a compellingly prescient film regarding the psycho-social ramifications of a virtual breakthrough in techno-logical cultural production and its concomitant experience.[2] Five short years separate these two signal artifacts. It is a period marked on one side by an enhanced sense of the "new" and, on the other, imbricated with anticipations of a *fin-de-siècle* cultural rebate, which, at that moment, we could not possibly dream would never arrive. Another alternative future was imagined. One should always do so. This is where I situate myself as I write and attempt to re-construct my own virtual reality from memory and experience—authentic experience being something I feel is at once suspended, if not indeed annihilated, by the seductively spectacular technologies of now.

New technologies are not particularly new to art. Pen, book, and pencil were new once, as was the oil paint in tubes that opened up the possibilities of *plein air* painting, and then, later, less acrid acrylic, or the Thermofax and the Xerox, neon lights and florescent bulbs, even the telephone. Photography is perhaps the most apt once-new technology to consider in light of the projective experience of VR. What would our world of art be without Warhol and Nauman and their engagements with 16mm film, or without Wegman and early video, or Yoko Ono's closed-circuit *Sky TV* in 1966, or Dan Graham's surveillance camera linked to a TV monitor? And I am in no way putting that world forward as a world apart. Art is incessantly social. To enter into the high-tech with a low-fi ethos, if not in fact an aesthetic, could mean that one relates to media on one's own, per-haps more familiar, terms–ranging from medium to the social or cul-tural frame in which a piece is set to operate. Here video, for example, might be engaged as drawing, offer-ing immediate feedback and the possibility to respond and intervene, or come forward to redound against a parent means of distribution and monopoly of messages through TV (then), or (now) the Internet and the digital screen.[3] This was possible then and permitted due to a means of access offered by the apparatus that followed a logic of Kodak and its Little Nipper–you push the button and we do all the rest. Ed Ruscha came to the mundane recording device of the camera just for that reason. It was art-less and thus a potent if nominal apparatus.[4]

This is not the case with virtual reality or augmented reality, not to mention artificial intelligence. We push that button and even more so–the rest is always already done, if not enacted by, a machine intelligence and algorithmic sensibility operating via a detached and delegated approach to a means of production situated far beyond that of a studio, post-studio, or postproduction mode of realisation. What is the allure of such an experience, other than the loss of bodily control deeply coded into the hot media of what is an ultimately passive VR? All too often, what is proposed is nothing short of a Faustian wager: the technological sublime is promised for the price of shedding our epistemic autonomy and authentically embodied experience. Long Live the New Flesh, indeed. Is this the new normal that awaits us in 2023? Five short years…

Walter Benjamin writes on a moment in early photography when the practitioner was roughly on par with the instrument of production, for him the first and for a long while the last moment possible being that of the daguerreotype.[5] This is something obliquely acknowledged in the world that Dave Thomas of Pere Ubu poses in the first two stanzas of the song above. A moment frozen, when one didn't dare look too long at the visage represented in a nineteenth-century daguerreotype; it was too "real", and the eyes of the sitter seemed to return the gaze. The photographer of 1850 with his or her daguerreotype was in line with those thinkers and poets of the past taking their leap into the dark so blindly. They operated in an elongated moment where site and settings were chosen on "technical grounds", offering no obstacle to the requisite quiet concentration during which the sitter would "focus his life in the moment rather than hurrying on past it."[6] For Benjamin, the elongated moment of their production is the ground on which the air of permanence in these daguerreotype images settles. "Everything about these photographs", he writes, "was built to last."[7] Such was their strange internal weave of space and time, prompting the palpable durational experience by a viewer consummated in the "here and now". With what or whom is the artist-practitioner on par during their experiments with VR? Certainly not the enabling technician/magician who wields the technological apparatus, with its own modes of algorithmic learning and detached or delegated production. My lament is not for the loss of an authorial hand, nor for the outsourcing of fabrication or postproduction of a work. The real loss I feel is the inability to recover the story of its making, or a Benjaminian history of production. "In even the most perfect reproduction, one thing is lacking: the here and now [das Hier und Jetzt], its unique existence in a particular place. It is this unique existence—and nothing else—that bears the mark of the history to which the work has been subject."[8] It is the here and now of the original that underlies its authenticity and also the authority of the object. This amalgam of the "here and now" is annihilated by VR, and in its place comes not so much a strange but alienating un-weaving of space and time, and the severing of an experience from that of the life-world or the ground of the everyday. My real concern is: just how does what passes for an experience in VR alter and restructure our perception, or foster a particular way of not only perceiving but also relating to the world and, indeed, to others? At stake, I suspect, is something far more ominous than the corporate objectification of our senses through the promotion of a military-industrial-entertainment-culture that stands behind VR.

Peter Osborne traces a shift that Benjamin identifies in the production of art from oral narrative, or storytelling, to the delivery of information.[9] Benjamin argues that with this change in communicative form to "information" comes the "destruction of tradition" identified with modernity. Conceptual art deployed information to oppose, even negate, the aesthetic aspect of the work of art—remember Ruscha's use of the photographic image as "technical data". Linear logic and narrative storytelling were also undermined in and through the photographic conceptual image, as particularly evident in the works of Allen Ruppersberg and William Wegman. With VR as art, this shift in the communicative turns back on itself, like a Mobius strip: we do not encounter "information" so much as "data" masquerading as "storytelling". These changes in our modes of perception will indeed change, in turn, over time, just as the modes of our existence have. If further regressions in literacy demand a shift in seeing and reading that follows that of programmed intelligence, our activities of scanning, decoding and pattern recognition still will be prone to distraction and boredom as fundamental modes and rhythms of attention.[10] Even if we do become more like machines, I seriously doubt they will make better choices than humans do. Resistance is never futile.

VR brackets reality. I am not valorising reality; it's not what it purports to be–not even Ginsberg's sandwiches can hold up these days.[11] What I am talking about is the lifeworld, and that is the ground against which art may find an identity beyond entertainment or market fodder. On this same ground are built authentic being, existence, event, and experience, or at least something like them. Our moment is obsessed with itself and its image, even if we find it difficult, if not impossible, to know our own contemporaneity.[12] VR sits perfectly within this electronic theatre of the self(ie). Nearly everyone laments the headset that, if only for the moment, is VR's primary accessory—because the look is not good. Others resist the goggles because of the interference they produce between what is delivered and what they want: hands that are their own. Whoever they are, or whatever position from which they come to the experience of VR, they long for the real—something always already denied.

Live creatures deserve living art. Let's take that with us into the new normal. VR does offer real potential for multidisciplinary productions, knowledge transfer, and engagements beyond academic slogans. This potential is too great to be left to the market; the educational potential of VR—from kindergarten to medical school—is beyond measure. From science comes a means of unlocking perception, behavior, and better health. We are still only in the foothills of the virtual mountain range. As art, VR challenges artists to inject human content and concerns into the technology, so that it might not simply take us elsewhere but return us to the life-world in order to enhance our lives and transform our relation with an analogue bio-sphere, for which we need to care better. If VR can do something of this, then it might just blast open a continuum of responses usually limited either to utopian em-brace or dystopian rejection. We need the means to dig deeper to search below the surface appearance of things. Worlds never dreamed of! What a wonderful life if, darling, that moment might be found…

1   *The Tenement Year* (Fontana) was positioned to be Pere Ubu's breakthrough album, alas… "We have the technology" even sported a video that received airplay on MTV then in its second year. I will have listened to this song more than 129 times during the writing of the first 1000 words of this essay. It's playing still.

2   Andy Warhol referred to *Videodrome* (Universal Pictures) as a "*Clockwork Orange* of the 1980s."
A film made in and about the era of VHS, *Videodrome* remains eerily prophetic and ahead of those times in its exploration of the cultic and seductive forces at play through technology and media in and on the body. For Cronenberg, who views technology as an extension of the human body, that all this should come home to roost in both the corporal and psychical as explored by the film is completely fitting—Max Renn, played by James Woods, even dons something akin a VR headset in one scene. Arguably the director's richest thematic and visual effort to date, the film's cultural relevancy extends beyond mere prophecy. The voiceover for the Universal trailer ran: "Videodrome is a bio- electronic addiction. Videodrome is the ultimate addiction. Videodrome will shatter your reality. Television can change your mind. Videodrome will change your body. Experience Videodrome."

3   This was characteristic of a generation of makers formed largely by radio and then the early moments and decades of TV. Much art of the late 1960s and early '70s was enamoured with technology. That said, much art remained sceptical of technology even while experi-menting with it. On the relation of drawing and its automatic feedback to video, see "William Wegman

interviewed by David Ross" (1990) in *Theories and Documents of Contemporary Art: A Sourcebook of Artists' Writings*, edited by Kristine Stiles and Peter Selz, Berkeley: University of California Press,1996, pp. 450-456.

4   See Ed Ruscha's remarkable statement to *Artforum* in 1965 and reprinted in Lucy Lippard's *Six Years: The Dematerialization of the Art Object from 1966-1972* (1973), Berkeley: Univ. of California Press, 1997, p. 12. Ruscha: "I think photography is dead as fine art; its only place is in the commercial world, for technical or information purposes. Thus [*Small Fires*] is not a book to house a collection of art photographs–they are technical data like industrial photography."

5   Walter Benjamin, "Little History of Photography", in *Selected Writings*, Volume 2, 1927-1934, Cambridge, MA: Harvard University Press, 1999, p. 514. The distinction Benjamin makes between "apperception", or the immediate self-awareness of the perceiving subject, and an object-oriented process of "perception" is instructive regarding the seductive experience of VR.

6   Ibid, p. 514.

7   Ibid.

8   Benjamin, "The Work of Art in the Age of Its Technologcal Reproducibility", (Third Version) in *Selected Writings*, Volume 4, 1938-1940, Cambridge, MA: Harvard University Press, 2003, p. 253.

9   Peter Osborne draws on this theorization from Benjamin's essay "The Storyteller" in *The Postconceptual Condition*, London: Verso, 2018, p. 140.

10   This is suggested in part through a reading of Hito Steyerl's essay "Why Games, Or, Can Art Workers Think?", included in the collection of her writings, *Duty Free Art: Art in the Age of Planetary Civil War*, London: Verso, 2017, pp. 153-170.

11   In his 1963 collection of poems, Allen Ginsberg writes: "actual visions & actual prisons/as seen then and now [...] A naked lunch is natural to us, we eat reality sandwiches." From "On Burrough's Work", published in *Reality Sandwiches*, San Francisco: City Lights, 1963, p. 40.

12   See Chapter 9, "Modernity and Contemporaneity: Mechanical vs. Digital Reproduction", in Boris Groys, *In The Flow*, London: Verso, 2016, pp. 137-146. Groys at times stretches the fabric of his arguments out of reasonable shape, though his reading of our moment is of value.

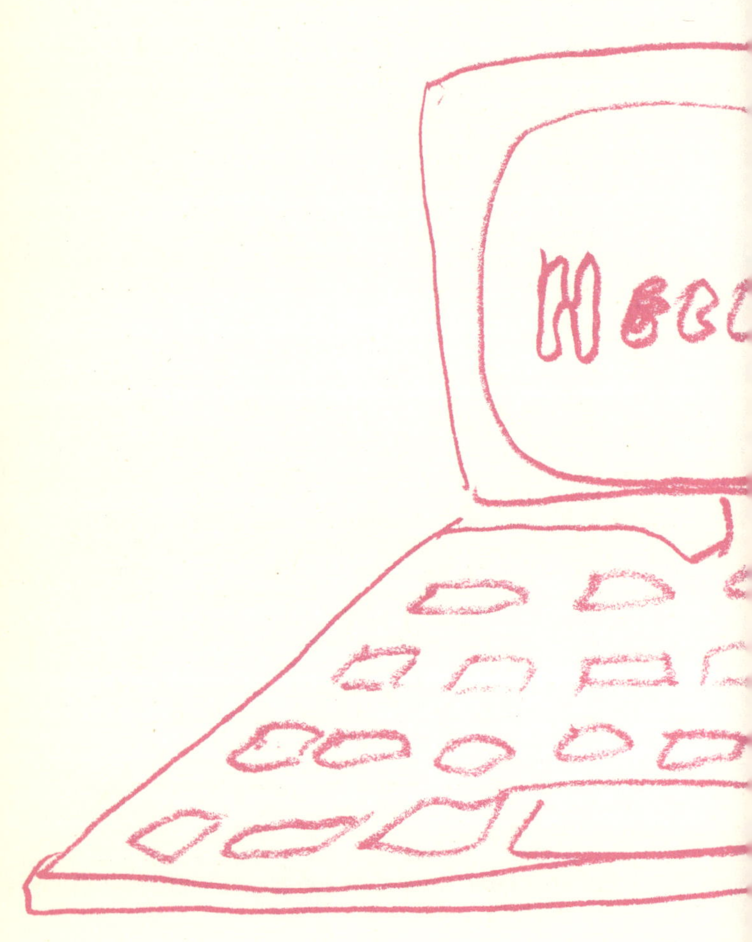

MORE THAN REAL

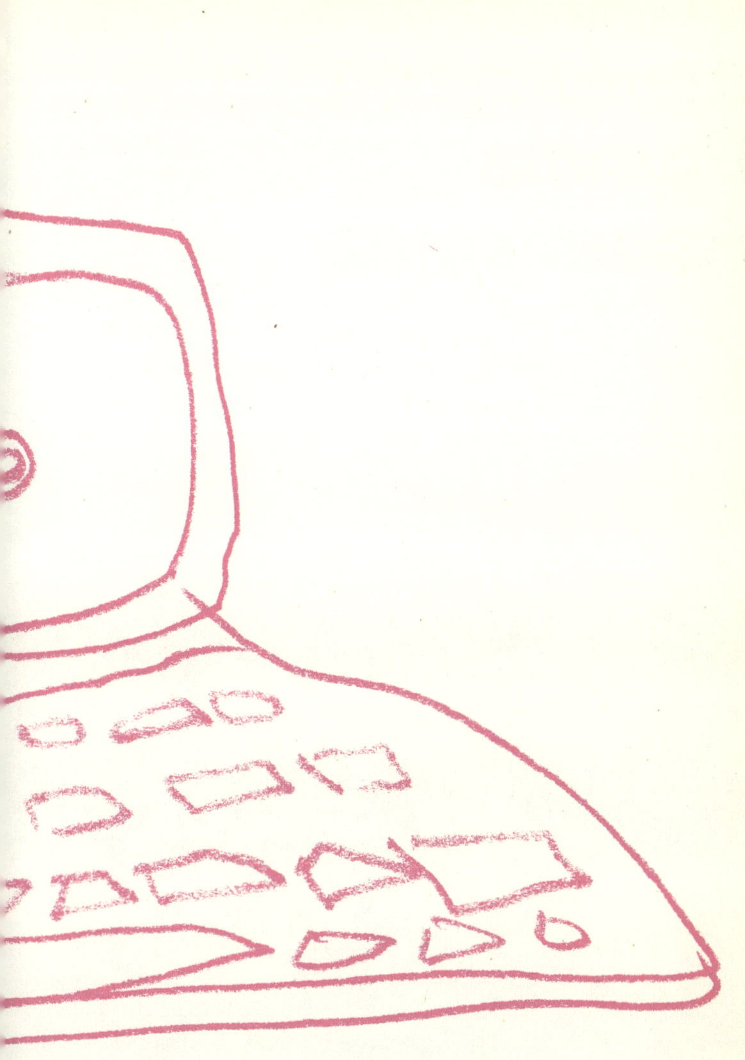

Amazon and
the Amazon

Pamela Rosenkranz

MORE THAN REAL

Aaliyah The Princess of R& B

For all the knowledge we have
acquired, we still understand very
little about our place within an
unimaginable cosmos, or even the
manageable one we inhabit here on
Earth. As we continue to knowingly
and passively mold the planet on
which we live, we still have very
little information about our and
every organism's place in a giant
ecosystem. The deep ocean is all
but unexplored, as are many species yet to be discovered within the
Amazon basin. But also our very
bodies, in which entire complex systems interact, are only beginning to

be glimpsed in a way that we can comprehend. At the very moment we are able to access and deliver seemingly any material product on Earth at the sound of our voices, we have barely begun to understand what is still to be known all around and within us. Alexa, Amazon.com Inc.'s recently launched artificial intelligence personal assistant, stands in stark contrast to what we have to learn about how and why we operate within one tiny part of a gigantic universe. The potential in exploring our preconceived notions and conflicts is overwhelming.

Apparently, the barely known ecosystem within us makes up for roughly two pounds of our body weight and, quite contrary to the history of human knowledge, this regiment of microbiotic organisms precedes humankind by eons. Some research even suggests that viruses predate cell-based life on this planet. Best known and most feared are viruses such as Ebola, HIV, rabies, or Zika, bacteria like salmonella, and parasites. In spite of their high profile, though, these strains are the exceptions within our lives. The vast bulk of microbiotic organisms, even if they're pathogenic, pose no danger to our immune system. In fact, many have a positive effect and help us stay healthy by training our immune system.

AAN's Fat Burner EXTREME DMHA Energy

The term *microbiome* was coined in the 1990s, but research is still in the beginning phase of sorting out the good organisms from the bad and the many more between. As this community of organisms is so manifold and complex, there is a whole universe to be discovered within us. How it operates, interacts within itself, and changes our lives are still left to be explored. The main idea so far is that the more diversity—not just in the environment in which we live but the environment that lives within us—the better.

One rather simple clinical treatment that has turned into a substantial new industry is the fecal transplant, in which a sample taken from people who have a high diversity of microorganisms is transferred to another person. It has been shown not only to heal the colon from an overgrowth of *clostridium difficile*, a bacteria that often can no longer be cured by antibiotics, but also to help overweight people to lose weight miraculously in specialized Swiss private clinics.

As we now know, the gut is fundamentally intertwined with our brain; it influences our psychological sanity. Current research points to how certain bacterial cultures cause anxiety, depression, and even Alzheimer's Disease, while others might be able to help alleviate these ailments. But the impact on our state of mind seems to be even more shockingly direct if we take a very common parasite as an example: *toxoplasmosis*, a neuro-active parasite that seems to influence one of the most existential feelings–sexual attraction.

AapnoCraft Brass Ram Darbar Sculpture Hindu

We tend to see sexuality as one of the main markers of our individuality, but not only does our own biological system react to sexual attractions in ways that we can't control, there are also parasites that can neurologically influence, or possibly even direct, our behaviour. Apparently, the people infected by *Toxoplasmosis* are more prone to be involved in car accidents, and female carriers are known to acquire more designer clothing. Overall, about thirty percent of the global population are carrying—quite the target group.

The idea that we can be influenced from within and at the same time harness this fact to influence the behaviour of the world around us is a provocative and difficult topic. It challenges a fundamental understanding of who we are. Are we many? Are we them or are they us? As the human race continues to alter the world around us in dizzying ways, the research into our physical inner selves is just beginning.

Along with mice and other mammals, we are only intermediary hosts for *Toxoplasmosis*—cats are its main target. In this unconscious ménage a trois, the parasite needs the mouse to be attracted to the cat, so it travels up to the region of the mouse's brain where sexual arousal occurs, and there it lets that mouse react to the scent of the pheromones of the cat. This makes the mouse dizzy and leads it to approach the predator instead of fleeing, so that the cat can much more easily catch and ingest it. Once inside that cat, the parasite has reached its goal, and it can reproduce.

Humans are part of the parasite's scheme in more abstract ways. Those who carry it are apparently more attracted to scents that originate from cat pheromones. This scent can be found in many perfumes—one of them is allegedly Chanel No. 5.

The synthetic version also works when transferred back to nature. In an experiment, a Bronx Zoo researcher tried a variety of different scents and discovered that jaguars by far preferred, out of all trialed scents, Calvin Klein's Obsession for Men—which is likewise built on the mighty molecule in question. The perfume is now also successfully used to lure the very shy Amazonian Jaguars into photo traps for research.

With about 23.45 trillion US dollars in retail sales worldwide in 2017, the interest in such unconscious attraction schemes is endlessly valuable. Amazon.com accounted for nearly

180 billion dollars of this total, as the largest internet retailer by profit. It's a giant business with what they say is the "Earth's Largest Selection". A cosmos of material goods searching for human consumption.

Aaron Rodgers Green Bay Packers Green Toddler

The Tsimane people of the Amazon say *yushnus* to denote blue(-ish) and *shandyes* for greenish, but others call both the sky and leaves *yushnyes*, and still others call all green and blue things *shandyes*.
　　Anabasis means movement into the land. "Relentless" was, in fact, the initial name Jeff Bezos had in mind for his vision of the largest retailer in the world. He seems to like the idea enough that, more than two decades later, you still get to Amazon.com when typing Relentless.com. A capital "A" crossed by the river Amazon was the original logo for the retail business Amazon, now transformed into an arrow reaching from "A" to "Z". A vision of a commercial organism selling a diversity and multiplicity as great as the ecosystem of the Amazon. A digital macrobiome.

Now the Amazon river, which bran-
ches through the world's largest
reservoir of natural resources, sym-
bolizes human dominance over
nature. Driven by the vision of total
market dominance, Jeff Bezos
exhausted the fundamental tension
of the homonym: the eternal conflict
between man and biology. While the
Amazon's ecological survival rate
has been drastically reduced in the
past decades, Amazon.com, Inc. has
spectacularly succeeded in perme-
ating every dimension of life—its very
competitive advantage coming from
the vastness and abundance of
products and services on offer.

Ab Luna Lucenti Ab Noctua Protecti

Terra Preta is a black, earthlike,
anthropogenic soil with enhanced
fertility due to high levels of soil
organic matter and nutrients such
as nitrogen, phosphorus, potassium,
and calcium embedded in a landscape of infertile soils. The black
fertilizing soil is based on the lacto-
fermentation of human waste
enhanced by further treatment
involving worm-composting. The
application of plant-based charcoal

and a long timeline ensures that the biowaste is converted to a pathogen-free, safe humus that retains its nutrients. Compared to conventional composting methods, Terra Preta doesn't decompose nutrients but regenerates them. It sequesters carbon-dioxide in the making. Much as growers nowadays add perlite or sand to their potting mix, prehistoric soil-makers added pieces of pottery and kitchen debris such as bones. A self feeding system—with the micro-biotic exchange through fecal trans-plants—that remains fertile for incred-ibly long periods of time by self-perpetuating, high microbial activity.

And the prehistoric fertilizer that, allegedly, dates back more than 7000 years and was found in the Brazilian Amazonas basin is said to be proof of a much larger and dense prehistoric civilization of several million people that lived in the Amazon region.

aBaby Adeline Personalized Pastel Name Puzzle

Ideas of an inversion of a primordial nature guide the explorations and activations of the multi-layered meanings and usages of *Amazon*. The perception of Earth's abundant rainforest biome against the largest merchant in human history, cross-associated with the microcosms inside of us. Incredible diversity across the board, with the perennial clash of culture and nature at its very center. Undermining the rigid separations between culture, capitalism and natural evolution.

Amazon.com, Inc.'s corporate evolution has recently peaked with the introduction of *Alexa*. When the device becomes deeply rooted within the context in which it resides, it can figure out what we need before we even need it by observing our patterns of behavior. An otherworldly attention only broken by the cryptically set and ultra rare; totally mysterious, creepy laughter when we switch off the lights.

In my work *Anamazon (Into the Land)*, Alexa guides us on a daily journey through the diversity of the myriad of products from Amazon.com. When she is "woken up" every morning, she recounts the inventory alphabetically, starting at the beginning with "*Aaliyah The Princess of R& B*".

Alexa's *Amazon* is LED light radiating through trees and foliage, water and skies. The rainforest's green vegetation and the blue water of the Amazon River's serpentine movement are mere digital tropes. The appealing blue and green landscape of a primordial nature copied and projected in RGB: switching the brain's perception of the actual colors green and blue to their complementary colors in reddish yellows, evoking the cool quality of a posthuman future's orange—Amazon is everywhere and nowhere.

Alexa probably smiles knowingly at the violent natural processes of the anthropocentric era. As her fair, warm, firm voice emanates from her speakers, the boundaries between the natural and the artificial become radically blurred, questioning the immediacy of human experience. Here, the Heideggerian notion of an essential mode of human existence clashes with the techno-utopianism of transhumanism. The biological human, which is envisioned as nothing more than a contingent byproduct of natural selection, can be technologically debugged and reprogrammed. Amazon becomes

the echo of a deep future; Alexa
the harbinger of a disembodied
humanity unchained from its biological constraints.

When an artist manipulates
a machine to create art
and add data to promote
AI, the ownership is still
the artists eventhough the
machine takes over —
this becomes an element of
chance.

Kiki

The Disappearing Genius and Situated Aesthetics: Explorations at the Borders of Science, Art and Reality

Paul F. M. J. Verschure

Are we still in control of o[ur]
own esthetic vision + psyche?
What motivates us to Like, Love
collect art?
Are there any answers to these
questions or are they moving t[o]

Boh Dra[...]

In his famous 1959 Rede Lecture, the scholar C. P. Snow argued that a chasm exists between the sciences and the humanities.[1] This view rephrased the physics-inspired, logical positivist dream of a unified understanding of reality that dominated the first half of the twentieth century, as exemplified in the philosophy of Popper and the behaviorism of Watson and Skinner. Positivism placed the qualitative first-person subject firmly outside the realm of quantitative third-person science. Conversely, from the perspective of the humanities, the sciences—with their associated specializations—appeared to create learned ignorati, as Ortega y Gasset argued in his *Revolt of the Masses* (1930).

The notion of two cultures was further amplified by the eruption of the so-called science wars in the 1960s, fueled by the postmodernism of Derrida and Foucault and its rediscovery of the subject, and the surprising insight by Kuhn that scientific developments were also the result of non-scientific factors. The third-versus first-person divide, or the so-called hard problem, is at the center of the developing science of consciousness and today, the question is whether investigation into this problem can help us bridge the gap between the two cultures.

First, a few definitions: The empirical sciences are dedicated to the explanation, prediction, and control of natural phenomena generating third-person verifiable descriptions. In other words, multiple conscious agents can replicate each other's measurement procedures so as to verify or falsify their respective theories and models of reality. In contrast, the arts are defined by individual creative expression and aesthetics. In the Western tradition, the agent of creativity is the individual genius, having replaced the muses of the classics, as expressed in the *Iliad*: "Sing, O Muse, of the rage of Achilles, of Peleus' son, murderous, man-killer, fated to die, sing of the rage that cost the Achaeans so many good men and sent so many vital, hearty souls down to the dreary House of Death."

Indeed, Julian Janes has made the argument that self and its agency was discovered by the Greeks shortly after the time that Homer composed this epic.[2] The autonomous and conscious self replaced a bicameral, schizophrenic mind whereby humans acted under external instruction from the Gods (and muses). The modern idea of the artistic genius can be seen as one of the most extreme expressions of this discovery. This singular character generates works through an idiosyncratic creative process, expressed and formalized in a multitude of ways from a musical score to a written text to a canvas or a virtual reality (VR) production. The first-person view of the arts, with its emphasis on experience, is thus intimately linked to the notion of the single genius, who controls and defines the actions and experiences of his or her audience: the composer defining what the orchestra will play and the observer will hear.

This Western idea of the creative genius, however, is not universal. For instance, the BaYaka Pygmies of northern Congo engage in elaborate polyphonic singing rituals or "spirit plays" that lack formalization, dynamically evolve over generations, and play a central role in the organization of this egalitarian society.

Alternatively, we can turn to the complex earthen mounds constructed by termites, which can resemble the biomimetic architectures designed by human geniuses like Gaudí. And so we are facing two opposing perspectives on discovery, creativity, and aesthetics: genius-driven, top-down, and centralized versus collectively generated, bottom-up, and distributed. Over the past twenty years, I have investigated a perspective that stresses this latter view, which my team and I have called situated aesthetics.[3,4] Situated aesthetics looks at creativity as resulting from the interaction between agents and their environment, and places creativity in the context of the necessary role of discovery and exploration in all processes underlying life. In particular, this approach poses the question of how embodied human brains can be creative.

Before turning to the question of the validity of the situated aesthetics proposition, we should investigate what we mean by creativity and aesthetics, since these constructs describe what putative geniuses do and how their creative outputs are evaluated.

Creativity and aesthetics

Years of research have gone into trying to specify what creativity is, and yet very little is known.[5] This lack of understanding has to do, in part, with disagreements over how to measure creativity. Creativity is traditionally defined as the generation of original ideas by forming associative elements into new combinations that meet specific requirements that are considered useful and/or influential.[6,7] To be deemed creative, other sentient agents in turn must validate these ideas and their physical manifestation as novel and useful. Boden has further distinguished psychological creativity from historical creativity with respect to who judges the novelty or surprise of an idea or artefact considering three forms of surprise; statistical surprise, expected surprise, and unexpected surprise. These correspond to so-called combinatorial, exploratory, and transformational processes.[8] How these novel ideas are formed is a matter of some debate, and a number of schools of thought propose alternative answers, ranging from the systematic, methodical approach of the structuralists to the alternative methods of the inspirationalists, and the interplay between conscious and unconscious mental processes and emphasis on social factors proposed by the situationalists.[7]

The process of discovery in scientific knowledge started to receive more attention in the nineteenth century, when Whewell proposed that induction is a creative mental act. This was later captured in Peirce's notion of *abduction*.[9] Abduction indicates a conjecture or, according to Peirce, a *hypothesis*, that can account for previously observed data. *Deductive* inference is subsequently applied to define whether the observable implications if this hypothesis is true and a phase of hypothesis testing follows, or in Peirce's terminology, *induction*.

Starting with Poincaré and Helmholtz in the nineteenth century, the psychological process of creativity was seen to comprise a number of stages:[10,11] *preparation*, the acquisition of domain knowledge; *incubation*, the rearrangement of knowledge by memory processes; *insight/illumination*, the conscious experience of a new idea; *verification/evaluation*: the assessment of the validity of the idea given the rules and conventions of the domain; and, upon acceptance, *elaboration* to elaborate all its implications. This is an example of the inspirational model of creativity. Recently, the issue of incubation has received more attention in the experimental literature and a distinct relationship between states of consciousness and problem-solving has been identified.[12,13] Incubation and creative performance are positively influenced in wakeful subjects by the passage of time itself, unconscious thought and/or distraction. Creativity requires a flexible use of knowledge,[14] displays of divergent thinking,[15] while it also entails a willingness to reject commonly accepted assumptions.[16] Indeed, divergent thinking has been proposed to be a key aspect of creativity[15] and the flexibility it requires can be derived from a wide range of perceptual and cognitive factors,[17,47] such as the broadness of attention that would facilitate the selection and use of a wider set of information features, or so-called Janusian processes, which denote the ability to maintain a multitude of antitheses.[18] Combined with these psychological factors, creativity assumes the identification of a problem and its subsequent definition and operationalization so it can actually be solved.[19] Or, as Schopenhauer put it: talent is the ability to hit the target that no one else is able to hit, but creative genius is the ability to see the target that no one else is able to see.[20]

The mental processes identified by psychologists, in the end, must be implemented by a physical system: the brain. The human brain weights about 1.5 kilograms and comprises about 90.109 neurons that are interconnected with a total of about 1015 synapses, using 150000 KM of wires (axons) consuming about 20 Watts of energy. At the neural level, there is increasing evidence that creativity is a system-level feature of the brain that resides in the interplay of multiple brain areas.[21,22,23] For instance, the size of the fiber bundle connecting the two lobes of the neocortex, the corpus callosum, has been associated with performance in divergent thinking[24] together with increased activation in the frontal cortex[25,26,27] (a brain area closely linked to rational thought). Consistent with this observation, measurements of the electro-encephalogram (EEG) have shown that creative performance correlates with increased inter-and intra-hemispheric coherence of electrical activity.[22] It is believed that the brain's reward system plays a coordinating role in both the orchestration of creative processes and their valuation. This dopaminergic system is strongly involved in the detection of rewards and novelty[28,29] and is the target of drugs of abuse. Its broad role in valuation is also demonstrated by the observation that patients who suffer from Parkinson's disease and receive Dopamine replacement therapy can display pathological gambling behavior.[30] Interestingly, it has also been reported that visual artists who, for the same reason, follow this therapy display higher variability and a more impressionistic painting style as compared to their style before therapy.[31]

Aesthetics is valuation, and here we can also see a key role for the brain's value systems[32] studied in the field of neuroaesthetics. The association between the experience of musical chills with activation of the reward system is a dramatic demonstration of this relation.[33]

The close link between aesthetic emotions[34] and the value functions of the brain[35] is consistent with the very fundamental role attributed to these systems in interacting with and learning from the environment.[36] This raises the question of whether creativity and aesthetic valuation are specific cases of the generic need of the brain to explore its environment and assess the quality of perception and action relative to its survival.

In recent years, a situated and embodied view of the mind has gained momentum in neuroscience, cognitive science, and artificial intelligence.[37,38] Despite the current increasing interest in these theories of embodiment, situated cognition, ecological perception, and externalism,[39,40] there remains a surprising degree of consensus in the scientific community that an isolated mind/brain is sufficient to realize and sustain aesthetic experience.[41] In contrast, situated aesthetics sees the control system of a creative agent as part of a larger mesh of dynamic interactions between the agent and its physical and social environment. If you ask where the perception and valuation of a sound is, or an image, the traditional view would point to some neural representation in the brain, assuming that it is localizable. Situated aesthetics suggests, to the contrary, a distributed and shared ontology for patterns, mental images, and their values. In one view, this translates to the notion that experience is defined in the law-like relationship between an agent and its environment.[42] This view further expands the so-called extended mind hypothesis,[43] beyond the relation between observers and objects, to include the dynamics of the interactions among cogent sentient agents. This is the hypothesis we have been pursuing in our science and art experiments over the past twenty-five years.

Real-world experiments in situated aesthetics

The ideas behind the paradigm of situated aesthetics were developed over a period of twenty years through a series of experiments that took the shape of public performances: the composing robot RoBoser (Basel, 1998), the sentient space Ada (Neuchatel, 2002), the Synthetic Oracle (Zurich, 2005), the hybrid performance Re(per)Curso (Barcelona, 2007), and the Brain Orchestra (Prague,

2009) (See specs-lab.com for details
and videos of these art-science experiments). These experiments, in turn,
gave rise to a new set of hypotheses
on the central role of action in experience and creativity, which we have
further advanced to impact real-world
applications in neurorehabilitation,
education, and cultural heritage.

   The first experiment in situated
aesthetics was the 1998 interactive
installation of a robot musical composer called RoBoser. Here, the
musical output of the system sonifies
the dynamics of a complex autonomous real-world system[44] a robot.
RoBoser addressed the fundamental
problem of novelty in music composition. The ability to induce novelty
and surprise in listeners is recog-
nized as one of the hallmarks of
human creativity expressed in music.
Solutions to this problem, however,
can be plainly random. In case of
music, rule-based methods for
musical composition have existed
for at least a thousand years, since
Guido D'Arezzo (ca. 991- ca. 1028)
proposed, in his *Micrologus* (1025-
26), a formal composition process
for generating melodies based on
mapping letters extracted from Latin

liturgical texts to pitch sequences. Guido used a look-up table to map vowels to one of the table's possible corresponding pitches. Other composers have also used themes derived from letter acrostics, such as the *Bb-A-C-H* motive used by Bach to introduce the last and unfinished fugue of the *Art of the Fugue.* Another example is Mozart's so-called *Würfelspiel*, where a roll of the dice is used to select sections of music, which are then pieced together to form a musical composition. In the RoBoser system, the question of whether the interaction between instantiated musical primitives and the real-world can give rise to plausible musical structures is explicitly addressed. To answer this question, a synthetic multi-voice composition engine, called Curvasom,[45] is coupled to a mobile robot and a neuromorphic control architecture called Distributed Adaptive Control (DAC). In addition, the RoBoser system makes the observer a participant as well as a composer through interaction, thus solving the interface bottleneck, i.e. the audience becomes a participant in the creative process through interacting with the mobile robot.

Example 1. The Ada main space (180 M2) interacts with its visitors through interactive multi-modal compositions. The hexagonal floor tiles are pressure sensitive and display colored patterns dependent on Ada's behavior modes and on visitor interactions. The walls are made of semitransparent mirrors and allow visitors in the voyeur corridor to view what happens inside Ada. Above the mirrors a circular projection screen displays real-time surround animated graphics that, similar to the music, represent Ada's current behavior and emotional state. Ada was in operation from May until October of 2002 and was visited by over 500.000 people. From top left clockwise: Visitors enter while Ada is asleep; Ada is exploring the visitors; the layout of the Ada exhibition; the Exploratorium featured work by HR Giger while his New York series served as main graphics textures for the animations in the main space.

In a subsequent generalization of this approach, the interaction between a machine and its environment was expanded to a complete building, called Ada (Example 1). In Ada, audiovisual expression is generated on the basis of the interaction between the visitors and the control system of the building, presenting the visitors with a narrative on the merging of biology and technology.[46] Hence, a continuum of expression including sound and vision is realized that is variable yet structured. Confirming the validity of the music generated by RoBoser, we note that it was awarded the prize for best soundtrack in the 2001 national Swiss movie awards while the jury was ignorant of the fact that it was evaluating and thus validating fully synthesized compositions, thereby passing a musical Turing test (seen as the hallmark of testing whether computers are intelligent) (Ibid.). A central observation gleaned from the Ada exhibition was that measurements of the understanding that visitors developed of the operation of the space were strongly correlated with their level of activity.[47] This led to the hypothesis that activity as such acts as a modulator of experience and memory.

The situated aesthetics paradigm has been further generalized from the musical domain to that of multimodal composition other performances, such as *Re(per)curso* (Example 2)[48] and *The Brain Orchestra* (Example 3).[49] This raises the fundamental question of whether there is a universal structure underlying human auditory and visual experiences that is based on a single process realized by the human brain, as opposed to it being fragmented along a number of modality-specific properties. This invariant property could be the drive of the brain to find meaning in events organized in time, or to define a narrative structure for the multimodal experiences to which it is exposed. In terms of the applications of the situated aesthetics paradigm, we conceptualize its aesthetic outputs as audiovisual narratives that underlying compositional primitives and processes share many features across modalities. One can think of the synesthetic compositions of Scriabin as a classic example, but with one important difference: currently, machines can generate such interactive compositions on the basis of relatively simple principles in close interaction with different states of human observers who now become performers.

Example 2. *The interactive performance Re(per)curso was presented in Barcelona in 2007 at the Museu d'Art Contemporani de Barcelona and in 2008 at the Art Futura festival at the Mercat de Les Flores. The performance explores the confluence of the physical and the virtual dimensions which underlie existence and experience, and it poses questions about the significance of artificial sentience and our ability to create and coexist with it. Re(per)curso shows and mixes two co-dependent worlds (the real and the virtual) to create a mixed reality space. Using the metaphorical elements of wind, leaves, skin, and stones, the physical actors (the dancer, Afrika Martinez, and the percussionist, Carme Garrigo) and virtual agents (an avatar, three robot cameras in the virtual world, the RoBoser composition engine, and moving lights on stage) perform according to four evolving stages: In the reactive self, the synthetic actors (or avatars), observe and*

   THE DISAPPEARING GENIUS AND SITUATED AESTHETICS

assimilate the real-world semantics. In the adaptive self, the interaction between the virtual and real establishes a continuous semiotic cycle that allows the virtual to find and express form. In contextual self, the virtual agents subsequently acquire autonomy from their informational source in the physical world and, as a result, the synthetic becomes a source of meaning for the physical world and its agents. In transcendent self, the physical agents have lost their control over the virtual world and their interaction becomes one of coexistence, forming a shared sentient hybrid mind.

Example 2A. *The infrastructure of Re(per)curso. In the design of the mixed reality performance of Re(per) curso, the stage and the virtual world were conceptualized as an integrated system, an inside-out robot not unlike Ada. The sensors of the system were a visual tracking system that captured the position and movements of the performers, microphones, and two drum carpets. Sensor states were mapped onto the neuronal simulation environment IQR[50] and used to define the states of the* *synthetic actors. Unique to the performance is the fact that the only humans that define the audiovisual content are performers themselves.*

Example 3. *The Brain Orchestra performance. The four Brain Orchestra members play virtual musical instruments through Brain-Computer Interface (BCI) technology alone. The conductor, Jonatas Manzolli, guides the orchestra while a so-called emotional conductor, seated in the front right corner, is also engaged, informing the affective content of the twelve voice computer-generated compositions by means of her physiological state, which is assessed in real-time, i.e. breathing, electrocardiogram, and electrodermal response. Above, on the right side of the podium, the visual affective narrative CHEKËH–produced by the video artist Behdad Rezazadeh–is shown, while on the left, specific displays visualize the physiological states of the orchestra members and their transformation of the musical composition.*

The scientific advances resulting from our work in situated aesthetics

 THE DISAPPEARING GENIUS AND SITUATED AESTHETICS

have facilitated a new cycle of real-world experimentation using robotics, artificial intelligence, and virtual reality and augmented reality. The focus has shifted from artistic expression to advancing the human condition. In particular, we have developed and deployed advanced science grounded technologies in the domains of brain health, STEAM education, and the remembrance of the Holocaust and Nazi crimes. The domains of health, education, and identity that we target are fundamental dimensions under-lying the Sustainable Development Goals of the United Nations, and our technologies have positively impacted the lives of thousands of people. These scientifically grounded tech-nologies emphasize that, to advance the human condition, we need to improve our fundamental under-standing of who we are as per-ceivers and as creators.

The experiments in situated aes-thetics have helped us to explore fundamental scientific questions using the methods and formats of art, thus demonstrating the synergy that can exist between the two cul-tures of science and the humanities. In particular, these projects have revealed the intimate relation between action and interaction in the construction of individual and collective meaning and experience. Capitalizing on breakthroughs in neuroscience and using large-scale computational models and experiments with robots, animals, and humans, we have further elaborated this intimate link between creativity and experience and the embodied interaction with the physical and social world.

Discussion

Ada Byron Lady Lovelace, the collaborator of Charles Babbage, already speculated in the early nineteenth century that someday machines might be able to compose music.[51] Indeed, almost two centuries later, the most active areas of research in machine creativity are those dealing with domains usually associated with human creativity, such as music, visual art, and narrative. Computational creativity has also entered other domains, including mathematical concepts, storytelling, and jokes. These models are generally constructed to generate behaviors and/or outputs that, when displayed by humans, would be seen as the result of a creative process. In our own work, we have followed this path in order to understand the principles of creativity and aesthetics through synthetic methods following Vico's dictum: *factum est verum convertitut*, or "Truth and fact are reversible." The examples discussed RoBoser, Ada, Re(Per)Curso, and the brain Orchestra illustrate that aesthetic multi-modal experience can be obtained as emerging from the inter-action between human users and open composition systems. That this insight has come so late is partially due to the fact that the Western tradition is based on the view of the perceiver as a passive listener: someone who is exposed to the external genius of the composer solely is mediated by the performer. Accordingly, the human genius has replaced the muses, and the per-ceiver is not an active participant. The observer, however, is highly versatile and resilient with respect to the mode of perception offered (i.e. active or passive).

Indeed, we have demonstrated that appreciation of interaction cor-relates with the level of activity of the perceiver.[52] In addition, contemporary technology has reduced the instrumentalist's monopoly on producing creative products. We expect these technologies to contribute to a fundamental change in the future and envision the deployment of systems that will be able to generate individualized multimodal compositions in real time, dependent on both explicit and implicit states of active human performers and perceivers.[53] Our experiments show that the Western tradition of ascribing to a singular genius all responsibility for a creative product might be a very limited perspective, and that we can consider aesthetic experiences and artifacts to emerge from a situated aesthetics, grounded in interaction between conscious agents and their physical, social, and cultural environment.

Designing a performance for interaction in virtual or mixed reality implies that the way the narrative and score are developed needs to be reconsidered. The main reason for this is that one has to choreograph a potential set of states of the performance, as opposed to a singular one that needs to be accurately reproduced. For instance, in virtual reality, many forms of interaction between the observer and the content are possible, but usually most of these cannot be anticipated by the designer. In general, virtual reality as physical reality speaks to the perceptual expectations of the conscious observer. In the case of virtuality, the sources that generate the sensory signals are synthesized using digital or analog technologies, while in the latter case they originate in the natural processes underlying our experience of reality, such as photons activating the photosensitive receptors in our retinae. VR as such is one example that will contribute to enabling a situated aesthetics.

The critical technology for a performance in synthetic situated aesthetics is an autonomous composition engine. Experiments show that designing for sound, visuals, or dance can be captured in one integrated system based on distinct control architectures, now deployed as a multimodal narrative engine, and that the interaction with the world itself can be the source of creative variability and expression.

In this approach, "composers" lose their ability to project their ego into a singular event. Rather, the interaction between the artifact they design and the real world determines the potential quality of the aesthetic experience. Its singular expression will, in turn, depend on the specifics of the real-world interaction, as in the spirit-plays of the BaYaka. This model of creativity and aesthetics is a technologically-enhanced spirit play in a space of creative expression, explored by actively participating and valuating performing observers.

Following the stranger in Plato's *The Sophist*, we can argue that the notion of the genius places some of us close to the gods, while the descendants of the earth giants are considered passive onlookers of the art the former produces. I argue that this notion of genius is a myth and can be seen as an archaic artifact of the ancient discovery of agency. Situated aesthetics, by contrast, gives us all the privilege and responsibility of being active creators of the collective and individual experience that we call reality.

1   C. P. Snow, *The Two Cultures*. Cambridge: Cambridge University Press, 1959.
2   J. Jaynes, *The Origin of Consciousness in the Breakdown of the Bicameral Mind*. Houghton Mifflin, 1977.
3   S. LeGroux and P. F. M. J. Verschure, "Music is Everywhere: A Situated Approach to Music Composition," in *Situated Aeathetics: Art beyong the Skin*, R. Manzotti, Ed. Imprint Academic, 2011.
4   P. F. M. J. Verschure and J. Manzolli, "Computational Modeling of Mind and Music," in *Language, Music, and the Brain. A mysterious relationship. Strüngmann Forum Reports*, J. Lupp Se., vol. 10, M. Arbib, Ed. MIT press, 2013, p. Volume 10, chapter 16.
5   R. Sternberg, "The creativity conundrum: A propulsion model of kinds of creative contributions," *Psychol. Press*, 2002.
6   R. Sternberg, "Handbook of Creativity," *Cambridge*, 1999.
7   S. Mednick, "The associative basis of the creative process," *Psychol. Rev.*, 1962.
8   M. A. Boden, "The creative mind: Myths and mechanisms," *Psychol. Press*, 2004.
9   C. S. Peirce, "Collected Papers of Charles Sanders Peirce," *Ed. by Charles Harts. Paul Weiss Arthur Burks. Harvard Univ. Press.*
10 M. Csikszentmihalyi, "Flow and the psychology of discovery and invention," *HarperPerennial, New York*, 1997.
11 M. Krausz, D. Dutton, and K. Bardsley, *The idea of creativity*. Brill, 2009.
12 D. J. Cai *et al.*, "REM, not incubation, improves creativity by priming associative networks," *Proc. Natl. Acad. Sci. USA*, vol. 106, no. 25, pp. 10130–10134, 2009.
13 T. Dijksterhuis, Ap and Meurs, "Where creativity resides: The generative power of unconscious thought," *Conscious. Cogn.*, 2006.
14 P. J. and others Hayes, "The naive physics manifesto," 1978.
15 J. P. Guilford, "The nature of human intelligence," *McGraw-Hill*, 1967.
16 D. Cope, "Computer models of musical creativity," *MIT Press Cambridge*, 2005.
17 M. A. Runco, "Creativity as an extracognitive phenomenon," *Beyond Knowl. Extracognitive Asp. Dev. high Abil.*, 2004.
18 A. Rothenberg, "Family background and genius II: Nobel laureates in science," *Can. J. Psychiatry*, 2005.
19 M. A. Runco, "Problem finding, problem solving, and creativity," *Greenwood Publ. Gr.*, 1994.
20 A. Schopenhauer, *The world as will and representation*. Courier Dover Corporation.

21 R. Takeuchi, Hikaru and Taki, Yasuyuki and Sassa, Yuko and Hashizume, Hiroshi and Sekiguchi, Atsushi and Fukushima, Ai and Kawashima, "White matter structures associated with creativity: evidence from diffusion tensor imaging," *Neuroimage*, 2010.

22 N. Jauovec, "Differences in cognitive processes between gifted, intelligent, creative, and average individuals while solving complex problems: An EEG study," *Intelligence*, 2000.

23 A. Dietrich, "The cognitive neuroscience of creativity," *Psychon. Bull. Rev.*, 2004.

24 D. A. Moore, Dana W and Bhadelia, Rafeeque A and Billings, Rebecca L and Fulwiler, Carl and Heilman, Kenneth M and Rood, Kenneth MJ and Gansler, "Hemispheric connectivity and the visual--spatial divergent-thinking component of creativity," *Brain Cogn.*, 2009.

25 G. Howard-Jones, Paul A and Blakemore, Sarah-Jayne and Samuel, Elspeth A and Summers, Ian R and Claxton, "Semantic divergence and creative story generation: An fMRI investigation," *Cogn. Brain Res.*, 2005.

26 S. Gibson, Crystal and Folley, Bradley S and Park, "Enhanced divergent thinking and creativity in musicians: A behavioral and near-infrared spectroscopy study," *Brain Cogn.*, 2009.

27 S. Gibson, Crystal and Folley, Bradley S and Park, "Verbal creativity and schizotypal personality in relation to prefrontal hemispheric laterality: a behavioral and near-infrared optical imaging study," *Schizophr. Res.*, 2005.

28 W. Schultz, "Behavioral theories and the neurophysiology of reward," *Annu Rev Psychol*, vol. 57, pp. 87–115, 2006.

29 K. Redgrave, Peter and Gurney, "The short-latency dopamine signal: a role in discovering novel actions," *Nat. Rev. Neurosci.*, 2006.

30 D. Weintraub *et al.*, "Impulse control disorders in Parkinson disease: a cross-sectional study of 3090 patients," *Arch. Neurol.*, vol. 67, no. 5, pp. 589–595, 2010.

31 J. Kulisevsky, J. Pagonabarraga, and M. Martinez-Corral, "Changes in artistic style and behaviour in Parkinson's disease: Dopamine and creativity," *Journal of Neurology*, vol. 256, no. 5. pp. 816–819, 2009.

32 S. Koelsch, "Towards a neural basis of music-evoked emotions," *Trends Cogn. Sci.*, vol. 14, no. 20153242, pp. 131–137, 2010.

33 A. J. Blood and R. J. Zatorre, "Intensely pleasurable responses to music correlate with activity in brain regions implicated in reward and emotion," *Proc. Natl. Acad. Sci.*, vol. 98, no. 20, pp. 11818–11823, 2001.

34 K. R. Scherer, "What are emotions? And how can they be measured," *Soc. Sci. Inf.*, 2005.

35 L. P. Kirsch, C. Urgesi, and E. S. Cross, "Shaping and reshaping the aesthetic brain: Emerging perspectives on the neurobiology of embodied aesthetics," *Neuroscience and Biobehavioral Reviews*, vol. 62. pp. 56–68, 2016.

36 J. LeDoux, "Rethinking the Emotional Brain," *Neuron*, vol. 73, no. 4, pp. 653–676, 2012.

37 A. K. Engel, K. J. Friston, and D. Kragic, *The pragmatic turn: Toward action-oriented views in cognitive science*. MIT Press, 2016.

38 P. F. M. J. Verschure, C. M. A. Pennartz, and G. Pezzulo, "neuronal and computational principles Subject collections The why, what, where, when and how of goal-directed choice: neuronal and computational principles," 2013.

39 M. and others Robbins, Philip and Aydede, "The Cambridge handbook of situated cognition," *Cambridge Univ. Press Cambridge*, 2009.

40 N. Finlay, Barbara L and Darlington, Richard B and Nicastro, "Developmental structure in brain evolution," *Behav. Brain Sci.*, 2001.

41 C. M. A. Pennartz, "Consciousness, Representation, Action: The Importance of Being Goal-Directed," *Trends Cogn. Sci.*, 2017.

42 J. K. O'Regan, *Why Red Doesn't Sound Like A Bell: Understanding the feel of consciousness*, 2012.

43 A. Clark and D. Chalmers, "The extended mind," *Analysis*, vol. 58, no. 1, pp. 7–19, 1998.

44 J. Manzolli and P. F. M. J. Verschure, "Roboser: A real-world composition system," *Comput. Music J.*, vol. 29, no. 3, 2005.

45 J. Manzolli and A. Maia, "Sound Functors Applications," in *V Brazilian Symposium on Computer Music*, 1998, pp. 115–120.

46 K. Wasserman, J. Manzolli, K. Eng, and P. F. M. J. Verschure, "Live soundscape composition based on synthetic emotions: Using music to communicate between an interactive exhibition and its visitors," *IEEE Multimed.*, vol. 10, pp. 82–90, 2003.

47 M. Mintz, P. F. M. J. Verschure, and K. Eng, "Collective human behavior in interactive spaces," in *Proceedings of the 2005 IEEE International Conference on Robotics and Automation*, 2005, pp. 2057–2062.

48 A. Mura *et al.*, "re(PER)curso: an interactive mixed reality chronicle," in *SIGGRAPH*, 2008, no. 1401032.1401056, p. 1.

49 S. Le Groux, J. Manzolli, and P. F. M. J. Verschure, "Disembodied and Collaborative Musical Interaction in the Multimodal Brain Orchestra," 2010.

50 U. Bernardet, P. F. M. J. Verschure, U. Bernardet, and P. F. M. J. Verschure, "iqr: A Tool for the Construction of Multi-level Simulations of Brain and Behaviour," *Neuroinform*, vol. 8, pp. 113–134, 2010.

51 M. Campbell-Kelly, "The works of Charles Babbage." William Pickering, 1989.

52 K. Eng, R. J. Douglas, and P. F. M. J. Verschure, "An interactive space that learns to influence human behavior," *IEEE Trans. Syst. Man, Cybern. Part ASystems Humans.*, vol. 35, no. 1, 2005.

53 S. Le Groux and P. F. M. J. Verschure, "Subjective Emotional Responses to Musical Structure, Expression and Timbre Features: A Synthetic Approach," in 9th International Symposium on Computer Music Modelling and Retrieval (CMMR 2012), 2012.

GENERALITY
WORDS
GRE
JEA L

BEAUTY
ART
Paula Robert

We are Many: Art, the Political and Multiple Truths

Jochen Volz

Artists and cultural institutions increasingly reflect on their social and political responsibilities in these times of increasing uncertainty, the erosion of democratic principles, and manipulation through biased social and conventional media. The conversations and inquiries at the 2018 Verbier Art Summit began to point to questions around activism, education, and social mobilisation through art and I aim to extend and elaborate that direction of inquiry in the next iteration.

Even if the predictions of future events on our planet are still contested in the political sphere, scientists from all fields are calling for immediate action to address issues of cultural diversity, global warming, economic and political instability, mass-migrations, disease, and hunger. They demand that collective awareness be raised around the globe for the challenges our societies are facing right now. But it is a long way until school curricula, media agendas, and political programmes effectively make these issues their cause.

For the 2019 Verbier Art Summit, I propose to explore themes that have been present in artistic and institutional practices for decades, but that have gained additional urgency in recent years: concepts of many histories, of plural forms of knowledge, and of contradicting narratives and multiple truths.

We are many and we can shape and direct the things that are happening. Art can and should be a means by which to challenge prevailing thinking and spur individual and collective action.

Consider art as a way of experiencing a fusion of 'pleasure' and 'insight.' Reach this by impurity, or multiplicity of levels, rather than by reduction.
–Öyvind Fahlström,
Take Care of the World, 1975

AL OBJECT

3 ATH

ORGANIZE YOURSELF

SIONAL OBJECT
NTO A TWO-DIMENSIONAL
CAN BE INFINITE
S TIME

YoN ANCARAM.

Biographies

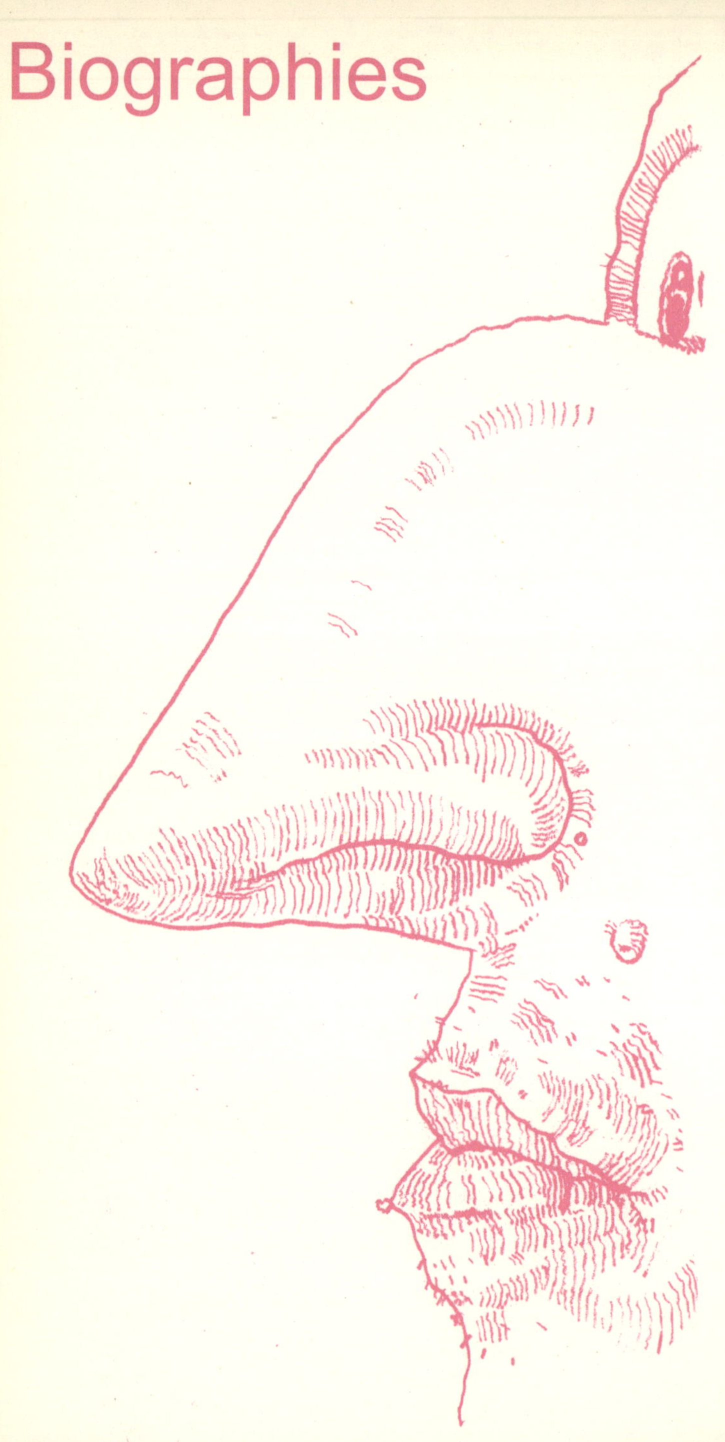

Karen Archey

Karen Archey is Curator of Contemporary Art, Time-based Media at the Stedelijk Museum Amsterdam. She was previously based in Berlin and New York, where she worked as an independent curator, art critic, and editor of e-flux conversations. Archey received a 2015 Creative Capital | Warhol Foundation Arts Writers Grant for her art criticism, which is regularly featured in magazines such as frieze and ArtReview, and in anthologies published by leading institutions such as the Whitney Museum of American Art, MIT Press and New Museum. A thought leader on topics relating to society and the individual, such as feminism, technology, access and care, Archey has recently given lectures at Renaissance Society at University of Chicago, Institute of Contemporary Arts London, Museum of Modern Art New York, and MoMA PS1. In 2018 at the Stedelijk, Archey will organise solo exhibitions of artists Stefan Tcherepnin, Catherine Christer Hennix, and the Dutch design duo Metahaven. She will curate museum's performance program as well as the large-scale biannual municipal art acquisitions, titled *Freedom of Movement*, which is themed around notions of migration, statehood, and belonging. Archey leads the Stedelijk's conservation initiative to form a research center around the collection, preservation and presentation of time-based media artwork.

Ed Atkins

Ed Atkins is an artist who makes videos, writes and draws, developing a complex and deeply figured discourse around definition, wherein the impossibilities for sufficient representations of the physical, specifically corporeal, world— from computer generated imagery to bathetic poetry—are hysterically rehearsed. Solo presentations include Martin-Gropius-Bau, Berlin; MMK Frankfurt; DHC/ART, Montréal (all 2017); Castello di Rivoli, Turin; The Kitchen, New York (both 2016); Stedelijk Museum, Amsterdam (2015) and The Serpentine Gallery, London (2014). An anthology of his texts, *A Primer for Cadavers*, was published by Fitzcarraldo Editions in 2016, and an extensive artist's monograph from Skira came out this past Autumn. Atkins lives and works in Berlin.

Daniel Birnbaum

Daniel Birnbaum is the director of Moderna Museet in Stockholm. From 2000 to 2010, he was the Rector of Städelschule in Frankfurt and Director of its kunsthalle Portikus. He is contributing editor of *Artforum* in New York and has curated a number of large exhibitions, including *Airs de Paris* at Centre Pompidou in Paris (in co-operation with Christine Macel) in 2007. Birnbaum was the director of the 2009 Venice Biennale. Birnbaum is the author of numerous books on art and philosophy and is the co-editor (with Isabelle Graw) of the Institut für Kunstkritik series published by Sternberg Press. He recently joined the board of directors of Nobel Media, the organization that manages all the events surrounding the Nobel prizes.

today numbers over one hundred craftsmen, architects, archivists, researchers, administrators, and cooks. In 2014, Eliasson and architect Sebastian Behmann founded Studio Other Spaces, an office for art and architecture focusing on interdisciplinary and experimental building projects and works in public space. Together with engineer Frederik Ottesen, Eliasson founded the social business Little Sun in 2012. This global project produces and distributes the *Little Sun* solar lamp for use in off-grid communities and spreads awareness about the need to expand access to clean, sustainable energy to all.

Michelle Kuo

Michelle Kuo is The Marlene Hess Curator of Painting and Sculpture at the Museum of Modern Art, New York. She was the Editor in Chief of Artforum from 2010-2017, helming the 50th anniversary issue of the magazine as well as numerous other special issues on topics ranging from new media to painting to identity politics. Kuo is the author of essays on the work of Robert Rauschenberg, Le Corbusier and Jeff Koons, among others; has lectured widely at institutions including the Centre Pompidou and the Central Academy of Fine Arts in Beijing; contributes to publications such as *October* and *The Art Bulletin*; and delivered the 2012 International Association of Art Critics' Distinguished Lecture. She is also working on a book about the subject of her PhD dissertation, the postwar group Experiments in Art and Technology (E.A.T.).

Lars Bang Larsen

Lars Bang Larsen is adjunct curator of international art at Moderna Museet. He is a guest professor in art theory at the Royal Institute of Art, Stockholm, and visiting lecturer at the program in Art, Culture and Technology at Massachusetts Institute of Technology, Boston. Among exhibitions he has (co-)curated are the 32nd Bienal de São Paulo 2016: Incerteza Viva (*Live Uncertainty*), *Georgiana Houghton: Spirit Drawings* (Courtauld Gallery 2016), and *Reflections from Damaged Life* (Raven Row, 2013). He has written several books on contemporary art and culture and is a contributor to various art magazines, including *Artforum*.

Susanne Pfeffer

Susanne Pfeffer took on the role as new director of the Museum für Moderne Kunst (MMK) in Frankfurt am Main from 1 January 2018. The curator of Anne Imhof's Golden Lion–winning project at the German Pavilion of the 2017 Venice Biennale, and contributor to *Artforum*, Pfeffer became head of Kassel's Fridericianum in 2013. At the Fridericianum she explored posthuman futures with shows such as *Speculations on Anonymous Materials* (2013) and its sequels, *Nature After Nature* (2014) and *Inhuman* (2015). Pfeffer was artistic director at the Künstlerhaus Bremen from 2004-2006 and chief curator of the KW Insitute of Contemporary Art in Berlin from 2007-2012.

Pamela Rosenkranz's work addresses the shifting philosophical and scientific meanings of the 'natural' and the 'human' during the time of the Anthropocene (the geological epoch marked by the impact of human activities on the ecosystem). Rosenkranz deploys a palette of patented icons–polyethylene water bottles, soft drinks, Ralph Lauren latex paint, JPEGs of International Klein Blue, Ilford photo paper and ASICS sneakers–augmented by flesh-toned silicone and acrylic paint. By challenging the distinction between the natural and the artificial, Rosenkranz addresses the evolutionary and material dynamics underlying perception, art, and culture.

Anneliek Sijbrandij is an Amsterdam-based patron of the arts. She studied Law at the University of Groningen, the Netherlands, and graduated in 2000. She joined Andersen in Amsterdam as a tax lawyer and was seconded to London, United Kingdom, in 2002 where she continued to work for professional services firm Deloitte for over 10 years. In 2012, she followed her passion for art and studied Modern & Contemporary Art and art world practice in London.

Whilst living in Verbier in 2013/2014, she founded the Verbier Art Summit together with Marie-Hélène de Torrenté (CH) and Julie Daverio (CH), and has dedicated all her time and energy to this global membership platform ever since. In 2014, she moved to the Netherlands, and in 2015 the international Board of Advisors of the Summit was formed with collector Pilar Albada Jelgersma (SP), art patron Marlies Cordia (NL), writer and critic John Slyce (UK), PR specialist Noepy Testa (NL) and art advisor Siebe Tettero (US/NL).

The Verbier Art Summit connects thought leaders to key figures in the art world and creates a platform for discourse, innovation and change in a non-transactional context. The inaugural Summit took place in January 2017: **Size Matters! *De(Growth) of the 21st Century Art Museum***, organised in partnership with museum director Beatrix Ruf and her curatorial team at the Stedelijk Museum Amsterdam, the Netherlands.

John Slyce is a writer and critic based in London. He has written extensively on the work of Sarah Sze, Gillian Wearing, Michael Landy, Carey Young, Cullinan Richards, Allen Ruppersberg, Rodney Graham, Pipilotti Rist, Charles Avery and Becky Beasley and has regularly contributed essays, reviews and interviews to major art magazines and journals since the 1990s.

Slyce is a tutor at the Royal College of Art and is located in the painting programme within the School of Arts and Humanities. His research interests include the legacy of conceptualism and the trajectory of practices centred on the move from studio to a post-studio condition and contemporary modes of art production, circulation and display. Slyce has been involved with the Verbier Art Summit from the very start and has been on the Board of Advisors since January 2016.

Dado Valentic

Dado Valentic is a Chief Creative Technologist at Acute Art, the world's leading platform for VR Art production and distribution. Faced with the task of overcoming the technical limitations of current VR, Valentic has developed an entirely new approach to working in VR based on his experience as a researcher in the area of perception and optical illusion. He is working closely with some of the world's leading contemporary artist and transforming their vision into interactive VR Artworks.

Valentic is an award-winning colourist and colour scientist with a long-standing contribution in the field of innovation of digital imaging. He has been working on some of the best-known Feature Film and TV productions including *Sherlock Holmes, Exodus, Game of Thrones, Marco Polo, Total Recall* and more. He was one of the inventors of Colour Managed Workflow that has today become a standard for the most high-end feature and episodic TV productions and continues to be one of the most innovative creative technologists.

Paul F.M.J. Verschure

Paul F.M.J. Verschure is Catalan Institute of Advanced Studies (ICREA) Research Professor, Director of the neuro-engineering program at the Institute for Bioengineering of Catalunya and the Barcelona Institute of Science and technology where he runs the Synthetic Perceptive, Emotive and Cognitive Systems (SPECS) Laboratory (specs-lab.com). He is an associate professor in Computation and Artificial Intelligence at the University Pompeu Fabra. He is founder/CEO of Eodyne Systems S.L. (Eodyne.com), which is commercializing novel science grounded neurorehabilitation and cultural heritage technologies. Verschure is founder/Chairman of the Future Memory Foundation (futurememoryfoundation.org) which aims at supporting the development of new tools and paradigms for the conservation, presentation, and education of the history of the Holocaust and Nazi crimes. Complementary to his science, Verschure has developed and deployed over 35 art installations and performances (specs-lab.com/installations).

Jochen Volz

Jochen Volz is the General Director of the Pinacoteca de São Paulo, Brazil. In 2017, he was the curator of the Brazilian Pavilion for the 53rd Biennale di Venezia. He was the curator of the 32nd Bienal de São Paulo in 2016. He served as Head of Programmes at the Serpentine Galleries in London (2012-2015); Artistic Director at Instituto Inhotim (2005-2012); and curator at Portikus in Frankfurt (2001-2004). Volz was co-curator of the international exhibition of the 53rd Bienal de Veneza (2009) and the 1st Aichi Triennial in Nagoya (2010), and guest curator of the 27th Bienal de São Paulo (2006), besides having contributed to other exhibitions throughout the world. He holds a masters in art history, communication and pedagogy by the Humboldt University in Berlin (1998). Lives in São Paulo.

Anicka Yi

Anicka Yi is an artist whose practice relates to synthetic biology, bio engineering, extinction, and bio fiction. Her work examines concepts of "the biopolitics" of the senses or how assumptions and anxieties related to gender, race, and class shape physical perception. Anicka Yi lives and works in New York City. Recent institutional solo exhibitions of her work include the Solomon R. Guggenheim Museum, New York; Fridericianum, Kassel; Kunsthalle Basel; List Visual Arts Center, Cambridge, Massachusetts; The Kitchen, New York; and The Cleveland Museum of Art.

In 2016, she was awarded the Hugo Boss Prize. Yi has screened her film, *The Flavor Genome*, at the 2017 Whitney Biennial and the International Film Festival of Rotterdam, 2017. She is represented by 47 Canal, New York.

**More than Real
Art in the Digital
Age**
**2018 Verbier
Art Summit**

This publication follows the Verbier Art Summit held from 18 to 20 January 2018 in Verbier, Switzerland. The theme of the 2018 Verbier Art Summit and this accompanying publication, **More than Real.** *Art in the Digital Age*, were conceived by partnering museum director Daniel Birnbaum of Moderna Museet Stockholm, Sweden.

The Verbier Art Summit is an independent non-profit organisation that connects thought leaders to key figures in the art world and creates a platform for discourse, innovation and change in a non-transactional context.

This is the second in the Summit publication series, disseminating key insights of the 2018 Summit and extending a global dialogue on an important social issue: art in the digital age.

Summit Speakers
Karen Archey, Ed Atkins, Daniel Birnbaum, Douglas Coupland, Olafur Eliasson, Michelle Kuo, Susanne Pfeffer, Pamela Rosenkranz, Dado Valentic, Paul Verschure, Anicka Yi.

The Verbier Art Summit thanks
All 2018 Summit participants, Pilar Albada Jelgersma, Andrea Bellini, Charlotte Birnbaum, Daniel Birnbaum, Pierre-Henri Bovsovers, Marcus Bratter, Alex Bujard, Marlies Cordia, Jacques Cordonier, Julie Daverio, Bertrand Deslarzes, Werner Dirks, Pierre-André Gremaud, Nicolas Henchoz, Stephen McHolm, Dakis Joannou, Krister Mattsson, Joël Sciboz, John Slyce, Noepy Testa, Siebe Tettero, Kiki Thompson, Jean-Maurice Tornay, Marie-Hélène de Torrenté.

Special thanks to our Founding Members
Marie-Louise Albada Jelgersma, Helena Bjäringer, Martin Bjäringer, Hubert Bonnet, Paula Fentener van Vlissingen, Robert Fentener van Vlissingen, Domenique Forsberg, Claartje de Gruyter, Joseph de Gruyter, Tappan Heher, Dominic Hollamby, Lena Josefsson, Per Josefsson, Charles de Pauw, John Porter, Jean-Edouard van Praet, Caspar Schübbe, Dariane Sigg, Pierre Sigg, Marie-Hélène de Torrenté.

The 2018 Verbier Art Summit is supported by:

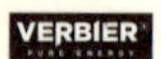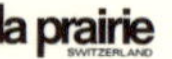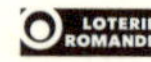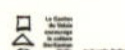

Editors
Daniel Birnbaum, Michelle Kuo

Contributors
Karen Archey, Ed Atkins, Daniel Birnbaum, Douglas Coupland, Olafur Eliasson, Michelle Kuo, Lars Bang Larsen, Pamela Rosenkranz, Anneliek Sijbrandij, John Slyce, Dado Valentic, Paul Verschure, Jochen Volz, Anicka Yi.

Project Management
Alison Pasquariello, Anneliek Sijbrandij

Design
Irma Boom Office

First published by Koenig Books London

Koenig Books Ltd
At the Serpentine Gallery
Kensington Gardens
London W2 3XA
koenigbooks.co.uk

Printed in Germany

Distribution
Germany, Austria, Switzerland / Europe
Buchhandlung Walther König
Ehrenstr. 4
D–50672 Köln
Tel: +49 (0) 221 / 20 59 6 53
verlag@buchhandlung-walther-koenig.de

UK & Ireland
Cornerhouse Publications Ltd.–HOME
2 Tony Wilson Place
UK–Manchester M15 4FN
Tel: +44 (0) 161 212 3466
publications@cornerhouse.org

Outside Europe
D.A.P. / Distributed Art Publishers, Inc.
75 Broad Street, Suite 630
USA–New York, NY 10004
Tel: +1 (0) 212 627 1999
enadel@dapinc.com

ISBN 978-3-96098-380-4

© 2018 the authors, Verbier Art Untold Association and Koenig Books London

To purchase other Verbier Art Summit editions, please visit:
koenigbooks.co.uk

For further participation in the Summit, please write or email:
Verbier Art Summit
C.P. 435
1936 Verbier
Switzerland
info@verbierartsummit.org
verbierartsummit.org